W9-BSM-406

Addison-Wesley's

Java Backpack
Reference Guide

Peter J. DePasquale
The College of New Jersey

PEARSON

Addison
Wesley

Boston San Francisco New York
London Toronto Sydney Tokyo Singapore Madrid
Mexico City Munich Paris Cape Town Hong Kong Montreal

Publisher	Greg Tobin
Senior Acquisitions Editor	Michael Hirsch
Editorial Assistant	Maria Campo
Marketing Manager	Michelle Brown
Marketing Assistant	Jake Zavracky
Senior Production Supervisor	Juliet Silveri
Copyeditor	Penelope Hull
Proofreader	Holly McLean-Aldis
Cover Designer	Joyce Cosentino Wells
Prepress and Manufacturing	Caroline Fell

Cover image © 2004 Photodisc

The tables on pages 6-11 are reproduced from Lewis/Loftus:*Java Software Solutions* 4th edition, Fig. 2.1, p. 67 (adapted from); Fig. 2.2, p. 74; Figs 2.5 and 2.6, p. 86; Fig. 3.2, p. 123 (adapted from); Figs. 5.1 and 5.2, p. 204; Fig. D.1, pp. 678-9; Fig. D.2, p. 680; Fig. E.1, p. 683; © 2005 Pearson Education, Inc. Reprinted by permission of Pearson Education, Inc., publishing as Pearson Addison-Wesley.

The help output in the gray boxes produced from command-line execution of Java programs is reproduced courtesy of Sun Microsystems, Inc.

Access the latest information about Addison-Wesley titles from our World Wide Web site: http://www.aw-bc.com/computing

Many of the designations used by manufacturers and sellers to distinguish their products are claimed as trademarks. Where those designations appear in this book, and Addison-Wesley was aware of a trademark claim, the designations have been printed in initial caps or all caps.

The programs and applications presented in this book have been included for their instructional value. They have been tested with care, but are not guaranteed for any particular purpose. The publisher does not offer any warranties or representations, nor does it accept any liabilities with respect to the programs or applications.

ISBN 0-321-30427-6
3 4 5 6 7 8 9 10-CRW-07 06 05

Acknowledgments

I deeply appreciate the comments, thoughts, and guidance of several people in writing this guide. Philip Isenhour, Deborah Knox, Cara Cocking, J.A.N. Lee, and Joseph Chase provided thoughtful input on a variety of topics, concepts, and presentation approaches.

Special thanks go to John Lewis for enlightening me on the teaching lifestyle, encouraging my ideas, and being among my closest friends. Finally (even though he doesn't actually edit anything), Michael Hirsch's vision, input, and guidance made this effort possible. Thanks to all of you for your assistance and support.

Dedication

I dedicate this work to my parents, Peter and Penny. They always believed I could be anything I wanted to be but encouraged me to do something other than teaching. It is ironic that teaching is what I returned to and enjoy the most.

Note

In summarizing the syntax of each reserved word, I have attempted to be brief and on topic. It should be noted that this guide is targeted for first-year programming students.

When portions of the syntax are optional, they are enclosed in brackets. In places where additional statements would be placed, such as the body of a method or a class, ellipses (…) have been substituted. Example:

[*modifier*] [**abstract**] *return-type method-name* ([*parameter-declarations*])   { … }

In this example, the abstract reserved word is highlighted for the discussion of its syntax and functionality. Though abstract is a modifier, other modifiers may also exist (e.g., *public, private*) in this type of statement; hence the [modifier] notation is also present.

Contents

Commonly Used Java API Classes and Interfaces

Java Fundamentals

Java Escape Sequences

Escape Sequence	Meaning
\'	single quote
\"	double quote
\\	backslash
\b	backspace
\n	newline
\r	carriage return
\t	tab
\f	formfeed
\000 to \377	Octal escape characters, equivalent to the Unicode values \u0000 to \u00FF.
\uXXXX to \uXXXX	Unicode characters (where each "X" is a hexidecimal digit [0–9, a–f, or A–F])

Java Numeric Primitive Types

Type	Storage	Minimum Value	Maximum Value
byte	8 bits	−128	127
short	16 bits	−32,768	32,767
int	32 bits	−2,147,483,648	2,147,483,647
long	64 bits	−9,233,372,036,854,775,808	9,233,372,036,854,775,807
float	32 bits	Approximately −3.4E+38 w/ 7 significant digits	Approximately 3.4E+38 w/ 7 significant digits
double	64 bits	Approximately −1.7E+308 w/ 15 significant digits	Approximately 1.7E+308 w/ 15 significant digits

Java Reserved Literals

Java contains three literal values, which are reserved for special meanings. The literal values "true" and "false" represent the only two possible states for a boolean value or expression. The "null" literal value is used to represent non-existent objects. These three literals are most often used in conjunction with equality operators or assignment statements. The "null", "true", and "false" literals may not be used as identifier names.

Java Logical Operators

Operator	Description	Example	Result
!	logical NOT	! a	"true" if a is "false," "false" if a is "true"
&&	logical AND	a && b	"true" if a and b are both "true," "false" otherwise
||	logical OR	a || b	"true" if a or b or both are "true," "false" otherwise

Java Equality and Relational Operators

Operator	Meaning
==	equal to
!=	not equal to
<	less than
<=	less than or equal to
>	greater than
>=	greater than or equal to

Java Bitwise Operators

Operator	Description
~	bitwise NOT
&	bitwise AND
|	bitwise OR
^	bitwise XOR
<<	left shift
>>	right shift
>>>	right shift with zero fill

Java Widening Conversions

From	To
byte	short, int, long, float, or double
short	int, long, float, or double
char	int, long, float, or double
int	long, float, or double
long	float or double
float	double

Java Narrowing Conversions

From	To
byte	char
short	byte or char
char	byte or short
int	byte, short, or char
long	byte, short, char, or int
float	byte, short, char, int, or long
double	byte, short, char, int, long, or float

Java Visibility Modifiers

Modifier	Classes and Interfaces	Methods and Variables
default (no modifier)	Visible in its package.	Visible to any class in the same package as its class.
public	Visible anywhere.	Visible anywhere.
protected	Not applicable.	Visible by any class in the same package as its class.
private	Visible to the enclosing class only.	Not visible by any other class.

Java Operator Precedence

In an expression, operators at a lower precedence level are evaluated before those at a higher level (first column). Operators at the same level are evaluated according to the specified association (fourth column).

Precedence Level	Operator	Operation	Associates
1	[]	array indexing	L to R
	.	object member reference	
	(*parameters*)	parameter evaluation and method invocation	
	++	postfix increment	
	--	postfix decrement	
2	++	prefix increment	R to L
	--	prefix decrement	
	+	unary plus	
	-	unary minus	
	~	bitwise NOT	
	!	logical NOT	
3	**new**	object instantiation	R to L
	(*type*)	cast	
4	*	multiplication	L to R
	/	division	
	%	remainder	

Precedence Level	Operator	Operation	Associates
5	+	addition	
	+	string concatenation	L to R
	-	subtraction	
6	<<	left shift	
	>>	right shift	L to R
	>>>	right shift with zero fill	
7	<	less than	
	<=	less than or equal to	
	>	greater than	L to R
	>=	greater than or equal to	
	instanceof	type comparison	
8	==	equal	L to R
	!=	not equal	
9	&	bitwise AND	L to R
	&	boolean AND	
10	^	bitwise XOR	L to R
	^	boolean XOR	
11	|	bitwise OR	L to R
	|	boolean OR	
12	&&	logical AND	L to R
13	||	logical OR	L to R
14	?:	conditional operator	R to L

Precedence Level	Operator	Operation	Associates
15	=	assignment	
	+=	addition, then assignment	
	+=	string concatenation, then assignment	
	-=	subtraction, then assignment	
	*=	multiplication, then assignment	
	/=	division, then assignment	
	%=	remainder, then assignment	
	<<=	left shift, then assignment	
	>>=	right shift (sign), then assignment	R to L
	>>>=	right shift (zero), then assignment	
	&=	bitwise AND, then assignment	
	&=	boolean AND, then assignment	
	^=	bitwise XOR, then assignment	
	^=	boolean XOR, then assignment	
	|=	bitwise OR, then assignment	
	|=	boolean OR, then assignment	

Summary of Selected Java Packages

Package	Functions
java.applet	Create applets
java.awt	Draw graphics and create graphical user interfaces (GUIs)
java.awt.Color	Create objects that represent and manipulate colors
java.beans	Develop JavaBeans
java.io	Perform input and output functionality. Utilizes buffers, streams, etc.
java.lang	General language support
java.math	Perform mathematical calculations and functions with high precision
java.net	Perform network communications
java.rmi	Perform Remote Method Invocation (RMI)
java.sql	Interact with databases
java.text	Format text for output.
java.util	General utilities (Random, Scanner, System classes, etc.)
java.util.jar	Perform reading and writing of JAR files
java.util.regex	Match sequences of characters against regular expression
java.util.zip	Perform reading and writing of ZIP and GZIP files
javax.crypto	Perform cryptographic operations
javax.swing	Create graphical user interfaces based on the java.awt package
javax.xml.parsers	Process XML documents

Common Java Executable Applications

- **appletviewer** – The Java **appletviewer** program permits the programmer to view and execute Java applets without the use of a full-fledged browser. The **appletviewer** provides a simple interface that contains the applet—suitable for debugging purposes. The URL or filename of the HTML page containing the applet is passed as a parameter to the appletviewer program.

> Usage: appletviewer <options> url(s)
>
> where <options> include:

-debug	Start the appletviewer in the Java debugger
-encoding <encoding>	Specify character encoding used by HTML files
-J<runtime flag>	Pass argument to the java interpreter

The -J option is non-standard and subject to change without notice.

- **jar** – The **jar** executable program is used to create, read, and expand Java archive files. Most often, **jar** files contain byte code files and other files required by the application at run-time (such as images for GUI buttons, icons, etc.). By manipulating the **jar** file's manifest file (META–INF/MANIFEST.MF), a **jar** file can be configured to be executable without the **jar** file being expanded.

Usage: jar {ctxu}[vfm0Mi] [jar-file] [manifest-file] [-C dir] files ...
Options:
-c	create new archive
-t	list table of contents for archive
-x	extract named (or all) files from archive
-u	update existing archive
-v	generate verbose output on standard output
-f	specify archive file name
-m	include manifest information from specified manifest file
-0	store only; use no ZIP compression
-M	do not create a manifest file for the entries
-i	generate index information for the specified jar files
-C	change to the specified directory and include the following file

If any file is a directory then it is processed recursively.
The manifest file name and the archive file name needs to be specified
in the same order, the 'm'and 'f' flags are specified.

Example 1: to archive two class files into an archive called classes.jar:
        jar cvf classes.jar Foo.class Bar.class
Example 2: use an existing manifest file 'mymanifest' and archive all the
        files in the foo/ directory into 'classes.jar':
        jar cvfm classes.jar mymanifest -C foo/ .

- **java** – The Java interpreter is the **java** executable program. This program is used to execute Java programs by interpreting the byte code files created from Java source code. Byte code files are created by compilation using the Java compiler.

```
Usage: java [-options] class [args...]
          (to execute a class)
or  java [-options] -jar jarfile [args...]
          (to execute a jar file)


where options include:
-client                     to select the "client" VM
 -server                    to select the "server" VM
-hotspot                    is a synonym for the "client" VM  [deprecated]
                            The default VM is client.
-cp <class search path of directories and zip/jar files>
-classpath <class search path of directories and zip/jar files>
                            A ; separated list of directories, JAR archives,
                            and ZIP archives to search for class files.
-D<name>=<value>            set a system property
-verbose[:class|gc|jni]     enable verbose output
-version                    print product version and exit
-version:<value>            require the specified version to run
-showversion                print product version and continue
-jre-restrict-search | -jre-no-restrict-search
                            include/exclude user private JREs in the
                            version search
-? -help                    print this help message
-X                          print help on non-standard options
-ea[:<packagename>...|:<classname>]
-enableassertions[:<packagename>...|:<classname>]
                            enable assertions
-da[:<packagename>...|:<classname>]
-disableassertions[:<packagename>...|:<classname>]
                            disable assertions
-esa | -enablesystemassertions
                            enable system assertions
-dsa | -disablesystemassertions
                            disable system assertions
-agentlib:<libname>[=<options>]
                            load native agent library <libname>,
                            e.g. -agentlib:hprof
                            see also, agentlib:jdwp=help and
                            -agentlib:hprof=help
-agentpath:<pathname>[=<options>]
                            load native agent library by full pathname
-javaagent:<classname>[=<options>]
```

> load Java programming language agent,
> see java.lang.instrument

- **javac** – The Java compiler is the **javac** executable program. It is used to compile Java source code files into byte code files for execution. The **java** executable program is used to execute Java byte code files (Java applications).

```
Usage: javac <options> <source files>
where possible options include:
  -g                       Generate all debugging info
  -g:none                  Generate no debugging info
  -g:{lines,vars,source}   Generate only some debugging info
  -nowarn                  Generate no warnings
  -verbose                 Output messages about what the compiler
                           is doing
  -deprecation             Output source locations where deprecated
                           APIs are used
  -classpath <path>        Specify where to find user class files
  -cp <path>               Specify where to find user class files
  -sourcepath <path>       Specify where to find input source files
  -bootclasspath <path>    Override location of bootstrap class files
  -extdirs <dirs>          Override location of installed extensions
  -endorseddirs <dirs>     Override location of endorsed standards path
  -d <directory>           Specify where to place generated class files
  -encoding <encoding>     Specify character encoding used by source files
  -source <release>        Provide source compatibility with
                           specified release
  -target <release>        Generate class files for specific VM version
  -version                 Version information
  -help                    Print a synopsis of standard options
  -X                       Print a synopsis of nonstandard options
  -J<flag>                 Pass <flag> directly to the runtime system
```

- **javadoc** – The **javadoc** executable program creates a series of HTML pages from a given set of Java source code files. Javadoc creates a programmer-friendly documentation set in the style of the Java API documentation.

```
Usage: javadoc [options] [packagenames] [sourcefiles] [@files]
  -overview <file>    Read overview documentation from HTML file
  -public             Show only public classes and members
  -protected          Show protected/public classes and
                      members (default)
  -package            Show package/protected/public classes
                      and members
```

–private	Show all classes and members
–help	Display command line options and exit
–doclet <class>	Generate output via alternate doclet
–docletpath <path>	Specify where to find doclet class files
–sourcepath <pathlist>	Specify where to find source files
–classpath <pathlist>	Specify where to find user class files
–exclude <pkglist>	Specify a list of packages to exclude
–subpackages <subpkglist>	Specify subpackages to recursively load
–breakiterator	Compute 1st sentence with BreakIterator
–bootclasspath <pathlist>	Override location of class files loaded by the bootstrap class loader
–source <release>	Provide source compatibility with specified release
–extdirs <dirlist>	Override location of installed extensions
–verbose	Output messages about what Javadoc is doing
–locale <name>	Locale to be used, e.g. en_US or en_US_WIN
–encoding <name>	Source file encoding name
–quiet	Do not display status messages
–J<flag>	Pass <flag> directly to the runtime system

Java Reserved Words

abstract (modifier)

Syntax

[*modifier*] [**abstract**] class *class-name*
    [extends *class-name*]
    [implements *class-name* [, *class-name...*]] { ... }

or

[*modifier*] [**abstract**] *data-type method-name* ([*parameter-declarations*])
    [throws *exception-type* [, *exception-type...*]] { ... }

Description

The **abstract** modifier can be applied to both classes and methods. In the case of classes, applying the **abstract** modifier prevents the class in question from being instantiated. **Abstract** methods must be implemented in a subclass. In both cases, the idea is that a subclass will provide the completed definition of the class or **abstract** methods.

Example

```
abstract class Motion {
    private int xDirection = 0, yDirection = 0;

    // The abstract move method must be implemented by an
    // appropriate subclass.
    abstract void move (int x, int y);

    // Returns the string representation of the two directions of
    // motion for this object.
    public String toString ( ) {
        return xDirection + ", " + yDirection;
    }
}
```

Tips

- Generally **abstract** methods are used for design purposes to specify that subclasses should provide the implementation of the method. In this situation, each multiple-child subclass can have its own specific implementation.

- If one or more **abstract** methods are present in a class, then the class itself must be **abstract**.

- A constructor cannot be modified with the **abstract** reserved word.

- **Abstract** methods cannot also be private methods.

- Interface classes are, by default, **abstract** in nature.

See also

- class (p. 26)
- interface (p. 44)

---

assert (control)

Syntax

assert *boolean-expression*;

or

assert *boolean-expression* : *expression*;

Description

The **assert** reserved word is used to test an assumption about a given boolean condition within your program. When used, **assert** is followed by a boolean expression that is verified before the code that follows is executed. If the assertion produces a "false" result, an AssertionException is thrown. If the assertion produces a "true" result, no exception is thrown and processing will continue as if the assertion were not present. In this manner, the assertion can be a very powerful programming construct.

Example

```
public class AssertTest {
    // A simple assertion test. Set a variable and then assert a known falsehood.
    // This code should throw an AssertionException. Be sure to execute the
    // code with the –ea switch on the command line.
    public static void main (String[ ] args) {
        int alpha = 5;
        assert (alpha < 5);
        alpha++;
    }
}
```

Tips

- Assertions may be inserted into your program and compiled, but by default they are disabled when executed. To enable the activation and testing of assertions, use the –**enableassertions** or **-ea** command line switch when executing your code. Example: **java –ea AssertTest**
- The second form of the **assert** statement (with two expressions) can be used to pass a value to the AssertionException's constructor, thereby providing additional information when the exception is thrown (and output is generated). The AssertionException's constructors accept a single value of the boolean, char, double, float, int, long, or Object types. In the latter case, the Object is converted to a string representation. Thus, our assertion could have been rewritten as **assert (alpha < 5): "alpha < 5";**

See also

- boolean (p. 19)
- false (p. 7)
- true (p. 7)

boolean (data type)

Syntax

[*modifier*] **boolean** *variable-name* [= *initial-value-expression*];

Description

The reserved word **boolean** is used to declare one or more variables of the **boolean** data type (containing a "true" or "false" value).

Examples

```
// Declares a boolean variable named found and sets its initial value to "true":
boolean found = true;
```

```
// Declares two boolean variables, minFound and maxFound, and sets
// maxFound's initial value to "false":
boolean minFound, maxFound = false;
```

Tips

- When declaring a **boolean** variable, you can optionally set the initial value of the variable by following the variable name with an equals sign and the initial value expression (as shown in brackets in the syntax statement).
- Multiple **boolean** variables can be declared in the same statement by following each variable name with a comma (see the second example).
- As class variables, booleans that are defined but uninitialized are assigned the default value of "false".

- As method variables, booleans must be initialized before being used.
- The java.lang.Boolean class is a wrapper class for the **boolean** primitive data type.
- Booleans cannot be cast to another data type, nor can another data type be cast to **boolean** values.

See also
- false (p. 7)
- true (p. 7)

- java.lang.Boolean (p. 67)

break (control)

Syntax
break [*label*];

Description
The **break** statement (when used without a label) stops execution of the enclosing switch, while, do, or for loop (known as the **break** target) and continues execution following the enclosing statement.

A **break** statement can include an optional label. When present, execution control is returned to the enclosing statement bearing the label.

Examples

```
// A switch statement involving an integer age variable. The break
// statement prevents the execution path from falling into the next case.
switch (age) {
    case 16:
        System.out.println ("Of legal driving age.");
        break;

    case 18:
        System.out.println ("Of legal voting age.");
        break;
}
```

```
// Search the class listing (String array of student names) for the presence of a
// specific target (String). If the target is found, the search terminates abruptly.
// Regardless of the search result, a boolean flag is set indicating the search result.
for (int index = 0; index < classSize; index ++) {
    if (classList[index].equals (target)) {
        found = true;
        break;
    } else
```

```
      found = false;
}
```

Tips

- If a **break** statement is not enclosed by a switch, while, do, or for loop, a compilation error will occur.

- If a **break** statement resides within a try block, the corresponding finally clause is executed before control returns to the **break** target.

- A **break** statement with a label is occasionally used to cease execution from deep within multiple nested loops.

- The use of a **break** statement (except when used in conjunction with a switch statement) is considered a poor programming practice.

- If the **break** statement is absent from the end of a case clause, execution will continue through the next **case** label and its statements (if present).

See also

- case (p. 22)
- do (p. 29)
- finally (p. 35)
- for (p. 38)
- switch (p. 56)
- try (p. 63)
- while (p. 65)

byte (data type)

Syntax

[*modifier*] **byte** *variable-name* [= *initial-value-expression*];

Description

The reserved word **byte** is used to declare one or more variables of the **byte** data type. In Java, bytes are 8-bit signed values. The minimum value of one byte is -128; the maximum value is 127.

Examples

```
// Declares a byte variable named alpha and sets its initial value to 19.
byte alpha = 19;
```

```
// Declares two byte variables, beta and gamma, and sets gamma's initial
// value to -5.
byte beta, gamma = -5;
```

Tips

- When declaring a **byte** variable, you can optionally set the initial value of the variable by following the variable name with an equals sign and the initial value expression (as shown in brackets in the syntax statement).

- Multiple **byte** variables can be declared in the same statement by following each variable name with a comma (see the second example).

- As a class variable, bytes that are defined but uninitialized are given the default value of zero.

- As a method variable, bytes must be initialized before being used.

- The java.lang.Byte class is a wrapper class for the **byte** primitive data type.

See also

- java.lang.Byte (p. 68)

case (control)

Syntax

```
switch ( expression ) {
    // One or more case clauses of the form
    [ case constant-expression:
        statement(s);
        [ break; ]
    ]

    [ default:
        statement(s);
        [ break ]
    ]
}
```

Description

The **case** label is used within switch statements to define executable blocks of code to be executed when the switch's expression evaluates to the **case** label's constant expression.

Examples

```
char letter = 'i';
String characterType = "unknown";

// Switch on the "letter" variable.
switch (letter) {
    // If "letter" is 'a', 'e', 'I', 'o', or 'u', set the type to "vowel."
    case 'a':
    case 'e':
```

```
    case 'I':
    case 'o':
    case 'u':
        characterType = "vowel";
        break;

    // Otherwise, set the type to "consonant."
    default:
        characterType = "consonant";
        break;
}
```

```
int value = 3;

// Switch on the value variable.
switch (value) {

    // If value is 1, increment by one.
    case 1:
        value++;
        break;

    // If value is 3, increment by two.
    case 3:
        value += 2;
        break;
}
```

Tips

- The constant expression must be a char, byte, short, or integer literal.
- Constant expressions within the same switch statement must be unique. One or more statements, terminated with a break statement, generally follow **case** labels. If the break statement is absent, execution will continue through the next **case** label and its statements (if present); **case** labels can also cascade through this mechanism, as shown in the first example.
- The default label can be used to define a block of statements (like a **case** label) that are executed if no **case** label matches the constant expression.

See also

- break (p. 20)
- default (p. 28)
- switch (p. 56)

catch (control)

Syntax

```
try {
    statement(s);
}
[ catch ( exception-type exception-identifier-name ) {
    statement(s);
} ]
[ finally {
    statement(s);
} ]
```

Description

The **catch** reserved word is part of the larger try/**catch**/finally statement. Each of these reserved words encloses a block of one or more statements that are executed under certain circumstances. The try block is executed first, until it completes execution of its statements or an exception is thrown.

If an exception arises, each **catch** clause is examined one at a time, in linear order, to determine whether the thrown exception matches a particular exception type. A match is made if the type of the exception thrown can be assigned to the type being caught. If a match does occur, the statement(s) in the matching **catch** clause are executed.

If an exception does not arise while executing the try block, processing will continue following the last **catch** block. If a finally clause is present, it will be executed; otherwise the next statement following the last **catch** clause is executed.

Example

```
// This method attempts to create a new File object from the specified filename.
// The object's creation and canWrite method may result in exceptions being
// thrown for several reasons.  Thus, two catch statements are required for this
// code to be compiled.
public void checkFile (String filename) {
    try {
        File inputFile = new File (filename);
        if (inputFile.canWrite ( ))
            System.out.println ("The file: " + filename +" can be written to.");
    }
    catch (NullPointerException nullPtr) {
        System.err.println (nullPtr);
    }
    catch (SecurityException securityExpt) {
```

```
        System.err.println (securityExpt);

    }
}
```

Tips

- A try block can have zero or more **catch** clauses associated with it, as long as a different type of exception is being caught by each clause. Keep in mind that different **catch** clauses can have exception types that are subclasses of each other.

- Generally, programmers use the **catch** clause to correct a potential error and proceed with processing. Some programmers use a **catch** clause to print a warning message or a trace of the program. In the event of a critical issue, it is possible to terminate the program abruptly within a **catch** clause.

See also

- finally (p. 35)
- try (p. 63)

---

char (data type)

Syntax

[*modifier*] **char** *variable-name* [= *initial-value-expression*];

Description

The reserved word **char** is used to declare one or more variables of the **char** data type (which contains character data values). In Java, chars are 16-bit unsigned values representing characters from the Unicode character set. Only 128 of the more than 65,000 character symbols that Unicode supports are traditionally used for programming and printing information in the English language.

Examples

```
// Declares a char variable named firstLetter and sets its initial value to 'p'.
char firstLetter = 'p';
```

```
// Declares two char variables, alpha and beta, and sets beta's initial value to '*'.
char alpha, beta = '*';
```

Tips

- When declaring a **char** variable, you can optionally set the initial value of the variable by following the variable name with an equals sign and the initial value expression (as shown in brackets in the syntax statement).

- Multiple **char** variables can be declared in the same statement by following each variable name with a comma (see the second example).

- As a class variable, chars that are defined but uninitialized are given the default value of '\u0000' (the null character).

- As a method variable, a **char** must be initialized before being used.
- The java.lang.Character class is a wrapper class for the **char** primitive data type.
- For more information on the Unicode character set, refer to the Unicode home page at http://www.unicode.org.

See also
- java.lang.Character (p. 69)

class (class-related)

Syntax

[*modifier*] **class** *class-name*
      [extends *class-name*]
      [implements *class-name* [, *class-name...*]]] {

    // Class variables, methods, and inner classes are defined here.
}

Description

The **class** reserved word is used to define the implementation of a class in the Java language.

Example

```
public class Student {
    // Stores the name and address of the student as Strings.
    private String name;
    private String address;

    // Returns the name of this student.
    public String getName ( ) {
        return name;
    }
}
```

Tips

- Classes can be declared within another class, thus giving rise to nested or inner classes.
- A **class** can inherit from another **class**—this is known as inheritance. Inheritance occurs by using the extends reserved word. A **class** can inherit from only one parent **class**.
- Classes that don't explicitly extend another class implicitly extend the Object class.

- An object can be created from the definition of a **class** by using the new reserved word.

- The definition of a **class** can be modified with one or more of the following: public, protected, private, abstract, static, final, strictfp.

See also
- abstract (p. 17)
- extends (p. 33)

- new (p. 46)
- java.lang.Object (p. 82)

const (unused)

Syntax
None; see Description.

Description:
The word **const** is a reserved word in the Java programming language, but it is currently unused.

Examples

None.

Tip
- If you are attempting to define a constant value, try doing so using the final reserved word.

See also
- final (p. 34)

continue (control)

Syntax
continue;

Description
The **continue** statement terminates processing of the current iteration of a loop at the point of the statement. This behavior is similar to that of a break statement, but rather than terminating the loop completely, the **continue** statement evaluates the loop condition and iterates again through the loop if the condition yields a "true" value.

Example

```
while (alpha < 5) {
    // Increment alpha and terminate this iteration of the loop.
```

```
alpha++;
if (alpha > 0)
    continue;

// The increment of beta is never executed.
beta++;
}
```

Tips

- In the example, the if statement was added to provide a possible path to the beta increment statement. Without the if statement, the compiler yielded a compilation error that the beta increment statement was not a "reachable statement" (because of the presence of the **continue** statement that always affects execution). By adding the if statement, the compiler cannot determine whether **continue** always affects the execution path (e.g., if alpha <= 0, **continue** is skipped).
- The **continue** statement can also be used in do and for loops.
- A compile-time error will occur if a **continue** statement is not enclosed by a do, for, or while loop.
- Care should be exercised when using the **continue** statement, as it may make source code more difficult to read.

See also

- do (p. 29)
- for (p. 38)
- true (p. 7)
- while (p. 65)

default (control)

Syntax
default:

Description
The **default** label is used within switch statements to define executable blocks of code to be executed in the event that the switch's expression fails to evaluate to any existing case label's constant expression.

Example

```
int value = 3;

// Perform a switch on the value variable, defined earlier.
switch (value) {
    // If value is 3, increment by two.
    case 3:
```

```
        value += 2;
        break;

    // The default case; increment value by one.
    default:
        value++;
        break;
}
```

Tips

- A **default** label is not followed by a constant expression, unlike the case labels also present in switch statements.
- The **default** label is generally listed last in the switch statement block. This helps distinguish it from the case labels. However, if the default label appears earlier in the list of labels, it does not impede the ability to correctly match case labels found later in the switch statement block.

See also

- case (p. 22)
- switch (p. 56)

do (control)

Syntax

do
    statement;
while (*boolean-expression*);

Description

The **do** reserved word is used to construct a loop that executes the specified statement one or more times until the expression following the while reserved word evaluates to a "false" value.

Example

```
// Continually loop and increase the value of alpha until alpha's value exceeds 5.
do
    alpha += beta;
while (alpha < 5);
```

Tips

- The statement portion of the **do** loop always executes at least once.
- If the boolean expression does not resolve to a boolean result ("true" or "false"), a compile-time error is generated.

- To execute multiple statements as the body of the **do** loop, enclose the statements to execute in braces, creating a statement block.
- Be sure that the boolean expression changes as part of the body of the loop. If the value of the expression does not change, the loop will be performed endlessly. This situation is known as an *endless loop*.
- Keep in mind that the boolean expression can comprise multiple boolean expressions, each joined by logical operators.
- A **do** loop may contain other loops (**do**, for, while), thereby creating nested loops.
- Break and continue statements can be used in **do** loops.
- A common mistake is to forget to insert a semicolon (;) following the boolean expression.

See also
- break (p. 20)
- continue (p. 27)
- do (p. 29)
- false (p. 7)

- for (p. 38)
- true (p. 7)
- while (p. 65)

double (data type)

Syntax
[*modifier*] **double** *variable-name* [= *initial-value-expression*];

Description
The reserved word **double** is used to declare one or more variables of the **double** data type. In Java, doubles are 64-bit signed values. The approximate minimum value of a **double** is –1.7E+308 and the approximate maximum value is 1.7E+308. A value of the **double** data type can contain up to fifteen significant digits.

Examples

```
// Declares a double variable named alpha and sets its initial value to 45.6964.
double alpha = 45.6964;
```

```
// Declares two double variables, beta and gamma, and sets gamma's initial
// value to -55.112D.
double beta, gamma = -55.112D;
```

Tips
- When declaring a **double** variable, you can optionally set the initial value of the variable by following the variable name with an equals sign and the initial value expression (as shown in brackets in the syntax statement).
- Multiple **double** variables can be declared in the same statement by following each variable name with a comma (see the second example).

- As a class variable, doubles that are defined but uninitialized are given the default value of zero.
- As a method variable, doubles must be initialized before being used.
- To reduce confusion between floating point literal values, **double** literal values can be appended with either the 'd' or the 'D' character (see the second example).
- The java.lang.Double class is a wrapper class for the **double** primitive data type.

See also
- java.lang.Double (p. 74)

else (control)

Syntax
if (*boolean-expression*)
    statement;
[**else**
    statement;
]

Description
The **else** reserved word is used to provide an alternative statement to execute in the event that an if statement's boolean expression resolves to "false". When used in conjunction with the if statement, a programmer can create an execution path for a "true" or "false" result in an if statement.

Example(s)

```
// Check to see whether the number of students in the course is equal to 25. If so,
// close this section. Otherwise, ensure that the section remains open.
if (numberOfStudents == 25)
    classFull = true;
else
    classFull = false;
```

```
// If the user-entered value is the string "Java", then print the names of two
// other OOP languages. Otherwise, print the names of two procedural languages.
if (enteredValue.equals ("Java")) {
    System.out.println ("Smalltalk");
    System.out.println ("C++");
} else {
    System.out.println ("Pascal");
    System.out.println ("Fortran");
}
```

Tips

- The **else** reserved word (and its corresponding statement) is an optional part of the if conditional statement.

- To execute multiple statements as part of the **else** clause of an if statement, enclose the statements to execute with braces, creating a statement block (see the second example).

See also

- false (p. 7)   • true (p. 7)
- if (p. 40)

---

enum (data type)

Syntax

enum *data-type* { *value1, value2, value3,* ... }

Description

The **enum** reserved word defines a new data type and corresponding values that the type may store. Identifiers created from this new data type can store only values listed in the data type's definition (*value1, value2, value3* in the syntax statement).

Example

```
public class U2 {
    // Define the Member data type and permit only the following values.
    enum Member {Bono, Larry, Edge, Adam};

    // Create specific identifiers for each band member and set their
    // appropriate values based on each member's role in the band.
    public static void main (String[ ] args) {
        Member vocals = Member.Bono;
        Member bass = Member.Adam;
        Member drums = Member.Larry;
        Member lead = Member.Edge;

        // Print the values of the membership of the band through
        // a variety of approaches.
        System.out.println ("Vocals: " + vocals);
        System.out.println ("Drums: " + drums.name ( ));
        System.out.println ("Lead Guitar: " + lead.ordinal ( ));
        System.out.println ("Bass Guitar: " + bass);

    }
}
```

Tips

- An enumerated type is a special type of Java class that also implements the Comparable and Serializable interfaces.
- The values of an enumerated type are stored as integer values. The first identifier is stored as a zero (0) value, the second as a one (1), and so on.
- The **name** method of an enumerated type can be used to obtain the string representation of an identifier's value.
- The **ordinal** method of an enumerated type can be used to obtain the numeric value associated with the identifier's value.
- Attempting to assign an invalid value (other than one of the specified possible values) to an **enum** variable will produce a compile-time error.
- Numeric values cannot be assigned to an enumerated type.
- A more advanced version of enumerated types permits the use of constructors, methods, and instance variables within the enum.

See also

- java.lang.Comparable (p. 72)
- java.io.Serializable (p. 85)

extends (class–related)

Syntax

[*modifier*] class *class-name*
    [**extends** *class-name*]
    [implements *class-name* [, *class-name*...]] { ... }

or

[*modifier*] interface *interface-name* **extends** *interface-name* { ... }

Description

The **extends** reserved word is used to modify a class's definition indicating that the child class is derived from the named parent class (class name).

Example

```
public class Rectangle extends Shape {
    ...
}
```

Tips

- Inheritance is the concept that one class is derived from another (existing) class.
- The existing class (Shape in the example) is known as the parent class, or superclass. The new class (also known as a derived class; Rectangle in the example) is known as the child class or subclass.

- In the Java programming language, a class can inherit from only one parent class. Thus, when using the **extends** reserved word, you never name more than one class to extend.
- Both abstract and interface classes can be extended.
- If a derived class does not extend itself from a parent class, the java.lang.Object class is the default parent class.

See also
- abstract (p. 17)
- class (p. 26)
- interface (p. 44)

---

final (modifier)

Syntax

[*modifier*] [**final**] class *class-name*
    [extends *class-name*]
    [implements *class-name* [, *class-name*...]] { ... }

or

[*modifier*] [**final**] *data-type method-name* ([[**final**] *parameter-declarations*])
    [throws *exception-type* [, *exception-type*...]] { ... }

or

[*modifier*] [**final**] *data-type variable-name* [= *initial-value-expression*];

Description

The **final** reserved word modifier is used to change the characteristics of classes, methods, fields, and parameters passed to methods (formal parameters). Generally, the use of the **final** reserved word implies that the item it modifies cannot be changed.

Example

```
public final class PI {
    // Sets the value of PI we use in this class.
    final double VALUE=3.1415;

    // Returns the area of the circle with radius rValue.
    public final double getRSquared (double rValue) {
        return VALUE * rValue * rValue;
    }

    // Returns the value of PI multiplied by the specified multiple.
    public final double getMultPI (final int mult) {
        return VALUE * mult;
```

```
        }
    }
```

- A class that is declared **final** cannot be subclassed or declared to be abstract.
- A method that is declared **final** cannot be overridden or declared to be abstract.
- A field (class or instance) that is declared **final** cannot be modified and must be initialized at the point of declaration.
- The **final** reserved word can be applied to formal parameters (parameters to a method) to prevent the parameter's value from changing.
- A constructor cannot be modified with the **final** reserved word.

See also
- abstract (p. 17)
- class (p. 26)

finally (control)

Syntax
```
try {
    statement(s);
}
[ catch ( exception-type exception-identifier-name ) {
    statement(s);
} ]
[ finally {
    statement(s);
} ]
```

Description
The **finally** reserved word is part of the larger try/catch/**finally** statement. Each of these reserved words encloses a block of one or more statements that are executed under particular circumstances as follows. The try block is executed first, until it completes execution of its statements or an exception is thrown.

If an exception arises, each catch clause is examined one at a time, in linear order, to determine if the thrown exception matches a particular catch clause. A match is made if the type of the exception thrown can be assigned to the type being caught. If a match does occur, the statement(s) in the matching catch clause are executed.

If an exception does not arise while executing the try block, processing continues following the last catch block. If an optional **finally** clause is present, it is executed; otherwise, the next statement following the last catch clause is executed.

Example

```
// This method checks to see whether the file specified can be written to.
// Note that the file is specified through a String parameter to the method.
public void checkFile (String filename) {
    File inputFile = null;
    try {
        inputFile = new File (filename);
        if (inputFile.canWrite ( ))
            System.out.println ("The file: " + filename + " can be written to.");
    }
    // Catches a possible NullPointerException from the File constructor.
    catch (NullPointerException nullPtr) {
        System.err.println (nullPtr);
    }
    // Catches a possible SecurityException from the canWrite method.
    catch (SecurityException securityExpt) {
        System.err.println (securityExpt);
    }
    finally {
        // If a File object was successfully created,
        // print its string representation.
        if (inputFile != null)
            System.out.println (inputFile);
    }
}
```

Tip
- Unlike the catch clause, there can be only one **finally** clause associated with a try/catch block.

See also
- catch (p. 24)   • try (p. 63)

float (data type)

Syntax

[*modifier*] **float** *variable-name* [= *initial-value-expression*];

Description

The reserved word **float** is used to declare one or more variables of the **float** data type. In Java, floats are 32-bit signed values. The approximate minimum value of a **float** is –

3.4E+8 and the approximate maximum value is 3.4E+38. A value of the **float** data type can contain up to seven significant digits.

Examples

```
// Declares a float variable named alpha and
// sets its initial value to 6.965.
float alpha = 6.965f;
```

```
// Declares two float variables, beta and gamma, and
// sets gamma's initial value to -12.345F.
float beta, gamma = -12.345F;
```

Tips

• When declaring a **float** variable, you can optionally set the initial value of the variable by following the variable name with an equals sign and the initial value expression (as shown in brackets in the syntax statement).

• Multiple **float** variables can be declared in the same statement by following each variable name with a comma (see the second example).

• As a class variable, floats that are defined but uninitialized are given the default value of zero.

• As a method variable, floats must be initialized before being used.

• To reduce confusion between floating point literal values, **float** literal values must be appended with either the 'f' or the 'F' character (see the examples).

• The java.lang.Float class is a wrapper class for the **float** primitive data type.

See also

• java.lang.Float (p. 75)

for (control; iterator-style)

Syntax

for (*collection-type loop-variable* : *collection-name*)
    statement;

Description

The iterator version of the **for** loop is a new language feature to Java 5.0. This form iterates over a collection of objects (collection name), visiting each object in the collection. While iterating, the object currently being visited is referred to as the loop variable. Each object in the collection is of a specified collection type. Using this form of the **for** loop, you can easily visit every item in a collection.

Example

```
// Prints the list of students (a list of String objects).
public void printList (ArrayList<Student> list) {
    for (Student member : list)
        System.out.println ("Student name: " + member);
}
```

Tips
- To execute multiple statements as the body of the **for** loop, enclose the statements to execute in braces, creating a statement block (see the second example in the traditional **for** loop summary on page 38).
- The new form of the **for** loop is also known as the **for**-each loop.
- The **for**-each loop can be nested inside another loop, and it also works with arrays.

See also
- for [traditional-style] (p. 38)

for (control; traditional-style)

Syntax
for (*initializer-expression*; *test-expression*; *update-expression*)
    statement;

Description
The **for** reserved word is used to construct a loop that executes the specified statement until the test expression evaluates to a "false" value. Before the first attempted execution of the loop, the initializer expression is executed (generally used to set loop control variables).

Next, the test expression is evaluated. If the test expression evaluates to a "true" result, the statement in the loop body is executed. Following each iteration of the loop, the update expression is performed and then the test expression is reevaluated. If the test expression evaluates to a "false" result, the loop terminates and control passes to the statement following the loop.

The initializer expression may optionally declare a variable and set its initial value (see the examples). If declared in the initializer expression, the variable is accessible only in the body of the loop; it is not accessible outside the loop.

The initializer expression and update expression may contain several expressions separated by commas (see second example). The test expression can comprise multiple expressions joined by zero or more logical operators.

Examples

```
// This loop is controlled by alpha (decreasing from 5 to 1).  Each time through the
// loop, the value of alpha is decremented and printed.
for (int alpha = 5; alpha > 0; alpha--)
    System.out.println ("alpha's value is: " + alpha);
```

```
// This loop is controlled by beta (decreasing from 5 to 1).  Each time through
// the loop, beta decreases by one, gamma increases by one, and the values
// of beta and gamma are printed.
for (int beta = 5, gamma = 0; beta > 0; beta--, gamma++) {
    System.out.println ("beta's value is: " + beta);
    System.out.println ("gamma's value is: " + gamma);
}
```

Tips

- To execute multiple statements as the body of the **for** loop, enclose the statements to execute in braces, creating a statement block (see the second example).
- Be sure that the boolean expression eventually changes as part of the body of the loop. If the value of the expression never changes, the loop will be performed endlessly. This situation is known as an *endless loop*.
- A **for** loop may contain other loops (do, **for,** while), thereby creating *nested loops*.
- Break and continue statements can be used in **for** loops.

See also

- break (p. 20)
- continue (p. 27)
- do (p. 29)
- for [iterator-style] (p. 37)
- while (p. 65)

goto (unused)

Syntax

None; see Description.

Description

The word **goto** is a reserved word in the Java programming language, but it is currently unused.

Example

None.

See also
None.

if (control)

Syntax
if (*boolean-expression*)
    statement;
[**else**
    statement;
]

Description
The **if** reserved word is used to build a conditional statement that may be used if the boolean expression is a "true" value. The statement is executed only if the boolean expression resolves to a "true" result. If the boolean expression is "false" and an else clause is present (following the statement), the else statement is executed.

Examples

```
// Check to see whether the number of students in the course is equal to 25.
// If so, close this section by setting the classFull flag to "true".
if (numberOfStudents == 25)
    classFull = true;
```

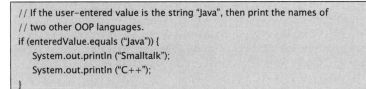

```
// If the user-entered value is the string "Java", then print the names of
// two other OOP languages.
if (enteredValue.equals ("Java")) {
    System.out.println ("Smalltalk");
    System.out.println ("C++");
}
```

Tips
- If the boolean expression does not resolve to a boolean result ("true" or "false"), a compile-time error is generated.
- To execute multiple statements when the boolean expression is a "true" value, enclose the statements to execute with braces, creating a statement block (see the second example).

- It is possible to nest **if** statements (the **if** reserved word, the boolean expression, and the statement). That is, an **if** statement can be executed as the result of another **if** statement.

See also
- boolean (p. 19)
- false (p. 7)
- true (p. 7)

implements (class-related)

Syntax
[*modifier*] class *class-name*
    [extends *class-name*]
    [**implements** *class-name* [, *class-name*...]] { ... }

Description
The **implements** reserved word denotes that a given class provides method implementations of the specified interface class.

Example

```
public class Student implements Undergraduate { ... }
```

Tips
- The **implements** reserved word can be used in conjunction with the extends reserved word to modify a class definition.
- A class can implement multiple interfaces by following the **implements** reserved word with a comma-separated list of interface class names.

See also
- class (p. 26)
- extends (p. 33)

import (class-related)

Syntax
import *type-name*;

or

import static *type-name.identifier-name*;

Description
The **import** declaration provides access to the specified class. In doing so, public static methods and data may be accessed by the file in which the **import** resides. Additionally,

the specified class may be instantiated (if permitted) by classes in the file in which the **import** resides.

Example

```
import java.util.Scanner;
import java.swing.*;
```

Tips

- By default, the java.lang package is imported to each class. Thus, there's never a need to **import** it explicitly. All other packages, however, need to be explicitly imported.

- The **import** declaration does not actually include the source code of the specified type name into the file that contains the **import** statement. Rather, it offers information to the compiler.

- When naming a class to **import**, you can substitute the name of the class with an asterisk (*) to indicate that you wish all classes from the package to be imported (see the second example).

- By adding the static reserved word between the **import** reserved word and the name of the class to **import** and appending a period and an identifier name, programmers can directly refer to static data fields contained in the imported class. Example:

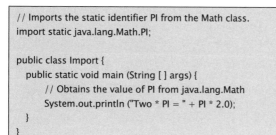

```
// Imports the static identifier PI from the Math class.
import static java.lang.Math.PI;

public class Import {
    public static void main (String [ ] args) {
        // Obtains the value of PI from java.lang.Math
        System.out.println ("Two * PI = " + PI * 2.0);
    }
}
```

See also
- static (p. 53)

instanceof (class–related)

Syntax
reference-name **instanceof** *class-name*

Description
The **instanceof** reserved word is an operator used to validate that a given reference to an object (reference name) is an instance of a specified interface or class (class name). A

boolean result ("true" or "false") is the result of an operation using the **instanceof** operator.

Example

```
// Verify that the miscObject is a String object. If it is, cast it back to a String
// and print its string representation.
if (miscObject instanceof String)
    System.out.println ("Student name: " + ((String) miscObject));
```

Tips

- The **instanceof** operator is frequently used to ensure that an object is of particular type before casting it to that type.
- Before the release of Java 5.0, this situation occurred most often when placing objects in a collection (list, stack, queue, and so on) that maintained a list of its contents as Objects. Removing one of the Objects from the collection resulted in the need be cast back to its true class before use. This validation check (using the **instanceof** operator) was generally present before the cast to ensure that a successful cast could take place. However, with the new generics type supporting collections in Java 5.0, this kind of cast has become obsolete.

See also

- class (p. 26)
- false (p. 7)

- interface (p. 44)
- true (p. 7)

int (data type)

Syntax
[*modifier*] **int** *variable-name* [= *initial-value-expression*];

Description
The reserved word **int** is used to declare one or more variables of the integer data type. In Java, integers are 32-bit signed values. The minimum value of an integer is – 2,147,483,648 and the maximum value is 2,147,483,647.

Examples

```
// Declares an integer variable named alpha and sets its initial value to 19.
int alpha = 19;
```

```
// Declares two integer variables, beta and gamma, and sets gamma's
// initial value to -5.
int beta, gamma = -5;
```

Tips

- When declaring an integer variable, you can optionally set the initial value of the variable by following the variable name with an equals sign and the initial value expression (as shown in brackets in the syntax statement).

- Multiple integer variables can be declared in the same statement by following each variable name with a comma (see the second example).

- As a class variable, ints that are defined but uninitialized are given the default value of zero.

- As a method variable, ints must be initialized before being used.

- The java.lang.Integer class is a wrapper class for the **int** primitive data type.

See also
- java.lang.Integer (p. 77)

interface (class-related)

Syntax

[*modifier*] **interface** *interface-name* extends *interface-name* {
    constant-definitions;
    abstract-methods;
}

Description

An **interface** defines one or more constant identifiers and abstract methods. A separate class implements the interface class and provides the definition of the abstract methods. Interfaces are used as a design technique to help organize properties (identifiers) and behaviors (methods) the implementing classes may assume.

Example

```
// The ShapeInterface defines two abstract methods for implementation by
// any shape. It also provides a weightMultiplier for use in various
// shape-related calculations.
public interface ShapeInterface {
    public final double weightMultiplier = 69.64;

    public int getArea ( );
    public int getCircumference ( );
}
```

Tips

- A class definition implements an **interface** through the use of the implements reserved word in its definition and through the implementation of the interface's abstract methods.

- An **interface** class cannot be instantiated.
- Methods contained in an **interface** class cannot contain statements. That is, their implementation must be left to the class that implements the **interface**.
- Multiple classes can implement the same **interface**, each providing differing definitions of the abstract methods of the **interface**.
- A class can implement more than one **interface** at a time.

See also
- abstract (p.17)
- class (p. 26)
- implements (p. 41)

---

long (data type)

Syntax
[*modifier*] **long** *variable-name* [= *initial-value-expression*];

Description
The reserved word **long** is used to declare one or more variables of the **long** data type. In Java, longs are 64-bit signed values. The minimum value of a **long** is

−9,223,372,036,854,775,808 and the maximum value is 9,223,372,036,854,775,807.

Examples

```
// Declares an integer variable named alpha and sets its initial value to 19.
long alpha = 19;
```

```
// Declares two integer variables, beta and gamma, and sets gamma's initial
// value to -55063L.
long beta, gamma = -55063L;
```

Tips
- When declaring a **long** variable, you can optionally set the initial value of the variable by following the variable name with an equal sign and the initial value expression (as shown in brackets in the syntax statement).
- Multiple **long** variables can be declared in the same statement by following each variable name with a comma (see the second example).
- As a class variable, longs that are defined but uninitialized are given the default value of zero.
- As a method variable, longs must be initialized before being used.
- To reduce confusion between integer literal values, **long** literal values can be appended with either the 'l' or the 'L' character (see the second example).
- The java.lang.Long class is a wrapper class for the **long** primitive data type.

See also
• java.lang.Long (p. 78)

native (modifier)

Syntax

[*modifier*] [**native**] *data-type method-name* ([*parameter-declarations*])
    [throws *exception-type* [, *exception-type…*]];

Description

The **native** reserved word is used to indicate that a method is called from the Java language but implemented in another programming language such as C++ or C.

Example

```
// Declares two methods that are native and implemented in another language.
public native int getAge ( );
public native void getAge (int newAge);
```

Tips

• Notice that the body of the **native** method is missing and only a semicolon follows the formal parameter list.

• A constructor cannot be modified with the **native** reserved word.

• **Native** methods cannot be declared as abstract or strictfp.

See also
• abstract (p. 17)   • strictfp (p. 54)

new (class–related)

Syntax

variable-name = **new** *class-name* ([*parameter-list*]);

Description

The **new** reserved word is used to create a **new** object (instance) of the specified class name. Generally, the instantiation is performed as the right-hand side of an assignment statement. The instantiation of the class executes the class's constructor and may contain zero or more parameters.

Examples

```
// Creates a new Integer object.
Integer result = new Integer ("45");
```

```
// Creates a new Student object by calling the default constructor.
Student freshman = null;
freshman = new Student ( );
```

Tips

- Objects can be instantiated without assigning them to variables. This event most often occurs when creating an object and passing it as a parameter to a method.
- Object instantiation does not necessarily need to occur in conjunction with variable declaration. It can be performed later and a reference assigned from the variable to the newly created object (see the second example).
- When instantiating an object from a given class (class name), a programmer makes a call to one of the class's constructors (methods with the same name as the class and with a void return type). The call to the constructor must match a constructor's parameter list (in order, type, and number of parameters).

See also
- void (p. 64)

package (class-related)

Syntax
package *package-name*;

Description
The **package** reserved word is used to place a class or interface into a specific organizational unit (package) named package name.

Example

```
package com.peterdepasquale;

// The Faculty class resides in the com.peterdepasquale package.
public class Faculty {
    String lastName;
    String firstName;
}
```

Tips

- If used, a named **package** must appear as the first item in a source code file, before import statements and any class or interface definitions.

- If a class is not placed in a specific **package** through the use of the **package** reserved word, then the class is placed in the unnamed (or default) **package**.

- Packages assist in the organization of the source code into modules of related functionality. Additionally, packages assist in preventing naming conflicts between types (classes).

- The general standard for naming packages is to use the components of your domain name in reverse order (e.g., edu.tcnj.depasquale).

- Subpackages can be created by appending additional components to the package name (e.g., edu.tcnj.depasquale.webSpider).

- It is considered good practice to name packages with a meaningful name.

See also

- class (p. 26)
- interface (p. 44)

---

private (modifier)

Syntax

[**private**] [*modifier*] class *class-name*
        [extends *class-name*]
        [implements *class-name* [, *class-name*…]] { … }

or

[**private**] [*modifier*] *data-type method-name* ([*parameter-declarations*])
        [throws *exception-type* [, *exception-type*…]] { … }

or

[**private**] [*modifier*] *data-type variable-name* [= *initial-value*];

Description

The **private** reserved word is used to modify the visibility of classes, methods, or data fields. In the case of a class, **private** visibility can be applied only to inner classes. Method and data field definitions can be modified with the **private** reserved word thereby preventing them from being accessed by subclasses. Additionally, **private** methods and data fields are inaccessible by any other class.

Example

```
public class PrivateExample {
    // The privateField data field is not inherited by subclasses and
    // is accessible only by instances of this class.
    private double privateField = 0.0;
```

```
// The incrementField method is not inherited by subclasses and is
// accessible only by this class.
private void incrementField ( ) {
    privateField += 3.1415;
}
}
```

Tip

- The use of **private** visibility helps promote encapsulation of the methods and data fields of a class. The selection of the visibility modifier for a class, method, or field is an integral decision of the engineering of software.

See also
None.

protected (modifier)

Syntax

[**protected**] [*modifier*] *data-type method-name* ([*parameter-declarations*])
    [throws *exception-type* [, *exception-type…*]] { … }

or

[**protected**] [*modifier*] *data-type variable-name* [= *initial-value*];

Description
The **protected** reserved word is used to modify the visibility of methods and data fields. Doing so modifies their access in several ways. First, **protected** methods and data fields are inherited and accessible by subclasses. Second, they are also openly accessible to any class in the same package as their class. Classes outside the package in which the method or data field is defined cannot access **protected** item(s).

Example

```
public class ProtectedExample {
    // This data field is inherited by subclasses and accessible by this class
    // and its subclasses.
    protected double protectedField = 0.0;

    // The incrementField method is inherited by subclasses and accessible
    // by this class and its subclasses.
    protected void incrementField ( ) {
        protectedField += 3.1415;
    }
```

}

Tips

- The use of **protected** visibility helps promote encapsulation of the methods and data fields of a class. The selection of the visibility modifier for a class, method, or field is an integral decision of the engineering of software.

- A class definition cannot be modified with the **protected** reserved word.

See also
None.

public (modifier)

Syntax

[**public**] [*modifier*] class *class-name*
        [extends *class-name*]
        [implements *class-name* [, *class-name*...]] { ... }

or

[*modifier*] [**public**] interface *interface-name* { ... }

or

[**public**] [*modifier*] *data-type method-name* ([*parameter-declarations*])
        [throws *exception-type* [, *exception-type*...]] { ... }

or

[**public**] [*modifier*] *data-type variable-name* [= *initial-value*];

Description

The **public** reserved word is used to modify the visibility of classes, interfaces, methods, and data fields in the Java language. When used with the definition of a class, **public** opens accessibility of the class to any other code (though the internal data fields and methods may have other visibility). Interfaces that are modified with the **public** reserved word are available to any other class.

Public methods are generally used to provide a service (e.g., accessors and mutators) to other classes. **Public** data fields are generally considered poor programming (unless they are also declared as final) because **public** data violate the notion of encapsulation of data within the encompassing class.

Example

```
public class Circle {
    // The value of PI is available to this and other classes but cannot
    // be changed.
    public static final double PI = 3.1415927d;
```

```
// The static area method returns the area of a circle, given a radius.  It
// uses the defined PI value.
public static double area (double radius) {
    return PI * radius * radius;
}
}
```

Tips

- If the constructor for a given class is non-**public** (private, protected, or without a visibility modifier), then only the class itself can make instances of the class.

- Non-**public** interfaces are visible only to classes within the same package as the interface.

See also
None.

return (control)

Syntax
return [*expression*];

Description
The **return** reserved word is used alone or with the optional expression to create a statement used to **return** execution to the calling method. When encountered, execution ceases in the current method and execution is transferred to the statement in the calling method or constructor.

Examples

```
// The getPostalCode method returns the postal code value (an integer)
public int getPostalCode ( ) {
    return postalCode;
}
```

```
// The setPostalCode method sets the postal code to the value specified
// and does not return a value.
public void setPostalCode (int value) {
    postalCode = value;
    return;
}
```

Tips

- If an expression is present in a **return** statement, the expression's resulting data type must match the data type specified to be returned according to the method's signature. That is, the expression must match the method's **return** type.

- Although it is possible to have multiple **return** statements, it is considered good programming practice to limit methods to containing one **return** statement.

- If a method does not **return** any data (the **return** type is void), a **return** statement need not be present. In the second example, it is present but returns nothing, so its presence does not cause any warnings or errors.

- Constructors can contain a **return** statement; but they must be devoid of the optional expression.

See also

- void (p. 64)

---

short (data type)

Syntax

[*modifier*] **short** *variable-name* [= *initial-value-expression*];

Description

The reserved word **short** is used to declare one or more variables of the **short** data type. In Java, shorts are 12-bit signed values. The minimum value of a **short** is −32,768 and the maximum value is 32,767.

Examples

```
// Declares a short variable named alpha and sets its initial value to 19.
short alpha = 19;
```

```
// Declares two short variables, beta and gamma, and sets gamma's initial
// value to -5.
short beta, gamma = -5;
```

Tips

- When declaring a **short** variable, you can optionally set the initial value of the variable by following the variable name with an equals sign and the initial value expression (as shown in brackets in the syntax statement).

- Multiple **short** variables can be declared in the same statement by following each variable name with a comma (see the second example).

- As a class variable, shorts that are defined but uninitialized are given the default value of zero.

- As a method variable, shorts must be initialized before being used.

• The java.lang.Short class is a wrapper class for the **short** primitive data type.

See also
• java.lang.Short (p. 86)

static (modifier)

Syntax
[*modifier*] [**static**] *data-type method-name* ([*parameter-declarations*])
    [throws *exception-type* [, *exception-type*...]] { ... }
or

[*modifier*] [**static**] *data-type variable-name* [= *initial-value*];
or

import **static** *type-name.identifier-name*;

Description
The **static** reserved word is used to modify a method or data field to be a class method
(or data field) rather than an instance method (or data field). That is, there will only be
one copy of the method or data field for all objects of the class that contains it.

Example

```
public class Course {
    // The static crsPrefix identifier is used in printing the TCNJ prefix.
    private static String crsPrefix = "TCNJ";

    // The getPrefix method returns the static data crsPrefix
    public static String getPrefix ( ) {
        return crsPrefix;
    }
}
```

Tips
• A **static** method can reference only **static** data and other **static** methods—it has no
  knowledge of instances of the class that contains it. All instances of a class can
  access instance data and instance methods as well as the **static** data and **static**
  methods of the class.
• If a **static** variable's value is modified, the change is seen by all of the instances of a
  class.
• A constructor cannot be modified with the **static** reserved word.

- Constant data fields (declared with the final reserved word) are often modified with the **static** reserved word to preserve memory. (Multiple copies of a value that cannot be changed are wasteful.)
- **Static** methods are generally used to provide a service to other classes. For example, see the public **static** methods contained in the java.lang.Math class, which contains a number of math-related service methods.
- The **static** modifier can also be used in conjunction with the import reserved word to import specific static identifiers from a specified package.

See also
- import (p. 41)

strictfp (modifier)

Syntax

[*modifier*] **strictfp** class *class-name*
    [extends *class-name*]
    [implements *class-name* [, *class-name...*]] { ... }

or

[*modifier*] **strictfp** interface *interface-name* { ... }

or

[*modifier*] [**strictfp**] *data-type method-name* ([*parameter-declarations*])
    [throws *exception-type* [, *exception-type...*]] { ... }

Description

The **strictfp** reserved word is used to modify a class, interface, or method, forcing it to use a strict calculation mode for all floating point calculations (those involving floats and doubles) performed within the enclosing block. Without the use of the **strictfp**, floating point expressions may take on an intermediate form that is larger than the allowable maximum (or minimum) value for the resulting data type.

With the strict floating point calculation mode in effect, intermediate calculations may not violate the maximum (or minimum) value for the data type. If the maximum (or minimum) allowable value is violated, the resulting expression will be "Infinity" (or "–Infinity" in the case of the minimum).

Example

```
public strictfp class Government {
    // The calcTaxes method calculates the amount owed based on
    // the annual salary provided. It utilizes strict floating point calculations.
    private strictfp float calcTaxes (float salary) {
        return salary * 0.338f;
```

```
        }
}
```

- When **strictfp** is applied to a method, all the code contained in the method is executed under the strict floating point calculation mode.
- When **strictfp** is applied to a class or interface, all the contained code is strictly evaluated.
- A constructor cannot be modified with the **strictfp** reserved word.
- Methods within an interface cannot be modified with the **strictfp** reserved word.

See also
None.

---

super (class–related)

Syntax
super._method-name_ ( );

or

super._variable-name_

Description
The **super** reserved word can be used in the nonstatic methods of a class to refer to its parent class. It may also be used to refer to data fields in a superclass.

Example

```
public class Beta extends Alpha {
    // The Beta constructor calls a constructor from Alpha that accepts one
    // integer value.  The super (without a method name) method call refers to a
    // constructor in the Alpha class.  The count variable contained in the
    // Alpha class is also incremented.
    public Beta (int value) {
        super (value);
        super.count++;
    }

    // This Beta constructor calls the getRandomValue method from the Alpha
    // class.  It will also print the value of the count data field from the super class.
    public Beta ( ) {
        System.out.println (super.getRandomValue ( ));
    }
```

```
}
```

Tips

- You can use the **super** reserved word to call a specific constructor in the parent class. If present, the call to the superclass's constructor must be the first statement in the subclass's constructor (as shown in the example).

- Methods or data fields existing in the parent class (which have been overridden in a subclass) can be accessed by the subclass by using the **super** reserved word. Use of this reserved word helps to specify which class a method call or field reference is referring to.

See also
None.

switch (control)

Syntax
```
switch ( expression ) {
    // One or more case clauses of the form
    [ case constant-expression:
        statement(s);
        [ break; ]
    ]

    [ default:
        statement(s);
        [ break ]
    ]
}
```

Description
The **switch** statement is used to provide an option for selecting and executing one of a number of paths. The selection is based on the result of the expression and the **switch** statement containing a case label for the path that matches the expression's result.

Examples

```
char letter = 'i';
String characterType = "unknown";

// Switch on the letter variable.
switch (letter) {
    // if 'letter' is 'a', 'e', 'I', 'o', or 'u' set the type to "vowel"
    case 'a':
    case 'e':
```

```
        // if 'letter' is 'a'. 'e'. 'I'. 'o'. or 'u' set the tvpe to "vowel"
        case 'a':
        case 'e':
        case 'I':
        case 'o':
        case 'u':
            characterType = "vowel";
            break;

        // Otherwise, set the type to consonant.
        default:
            characterType = "consonant";
            break;
}
int value = 3;

// Switch on the value variable.
switch (value) {
    // If value is 1, increment by one.
    case 1:
        value++;
        break;

    // If value is 3, increment by two.
    case 3:
        value += 2;
        break;
}
```

Tips

- The **switch** expression must evaluate to a byte, char, int, or short value.
- Any statement within the **switch** statement block must be labeled by a case or default label.

See also

- break (p. 20)
- case (p. 22)

- default (p. 28

synchronized (modifier)

Syntax
synchronized (*object-reference*) {

[*modifier*] **synchronized** *data-type method-name* ([*parameter-list*]) { ... }

Description

The **synchronized** reserved word is used to modify a method or to create a **synchronized** statement. In both cases, the result creates a method or block of code that is executable only by one thread at a time. Synchronization prevents concurrent access on a particular statement or block of statements.

In certain development situations (when working with threads), a programmer may wish to ensure that a given object is modified or referenced by only one thread at a time. In the example, we ensure that only one thread can call the addStudent method at any given time.

Synchronization is supported by a thread obtaining a lock on a given object reference (for **synchronized** statements) or enclosing class (for **synchronized** methods). If the lock cannot be obtained, the thread will wait until the lock can be secured. Completion of the **synchronized** method or statement results in the unlocking of a held lock. It is possible that a method or statement can prevent the unlocking (e.g., an endless loop), leading to the condition known as *deadlock*.

Example

```
import java.util.Vector;

public class CourseSection {
    // The enrollment vector holds a list of students in this course's section.
    private Vector<Student> enrollment = new Vector<Student> ();

    // Adds a student to this course's section.  The method is synchronized to
    // prevent multiple threads from executing the method at the same time.
    public synchronized void addStudent (Student enrollee) {
        if (enrollee != null)
            enrollment.add (enrollee);
    }

    // Removes the first student from the enrollment vector.  Code enclosing
    // the vector editing is synchronized to prevent multiple concurrent access.
    public void removeFirst ( ) {
        synchronized (enrollment) {
            enrollment.removeElementAt (0);
        }
    }
}
```

Tips

• A **synchronized** statement attempts to lock the lock associated with the named object reference.

- A **synchronized** instance method attempts to lock the lock associated with the instance of the class that contains the method.
- A **synchronized** static method attempts to lock the lock associated with the Class object (java.lang.Class) for the class that contains the method.
- A constructor cannot be modified with the **synchronized** reserved word.

See also
None.

this (class-related)

Syntax
this.*data-field*
or

this.*method-name* ([*parameter-list*]);

Description
The **this** reserved word in Java is used within an object to refer to itself. It is most often used in constructors and instance methods to refer to instance data fields that may have the same name as the formal parameters of the constructor or method. The **this** reserved word can therefore be used to clarify which variable (the formal parameter or instance data field) you wish to reference.

Example

```
public class Section {
    // The instance variables sectionNumber and sectionEnrollment keep track of
    // key information about each instance of a course's section.
    private int sectionNumber;
    private int sectionEnrollment;

    // The Section constructor accepts values for the section number and
    // the size of this section.
    public Section (int sectionNumber, int sectionEnrollment) {
        this.sectionNumber = sectionNumber;
        this.sectionEnrollment = sectionEnrollment;
    }
}
```

Tip
- The **this** reserved word is technically a reference to the current object. It can also be used as a parameter to a method. Example: enrollment.add (**this**);

See also
None.

throw (control)

Syntax
throw *expression*;

Description

The **throw** reserved word is used to cause an instance of an exception to be thrown. Thrown exceptions that are not caught by a catch block propagate upward through the calling method(s) until they are caught. If the exception is not caught, the exception's execution thread is terminated when it reaches the top of the calling chain (sequence of method calls).

Example

```
public class ThrowingTester {
    // The main method creates and throws a new RuntimeException
    // object if there are no command line parameters present.
    public static void main (String[ ] args) throws RuntimeException {
        if (args.length < 1)
            throw new RuntimeException ("command line parameters missing!");
        else
            System.out.println ("Hello " + args[0]);
    }
}
```

Tips

- The expression type in the **throw** statement must match one of the exception types in the throw clause (or be an instance of the java.lang.Throwable class or a subclass of Throwable) for the method that contains the **throw** statement.
- Not all exceptions are thrown by the programmer's source code. Some exceptions may be thrown as the result of run-time situations arising. The exceptions may include file-not-found exceptions, divide-by-zero exceptions, an out-of-memory error, or other unplanned situations.

See also
- catch (p. 24)

throws (class-related)

Syntax
[*modifier*] *data-type method-name* ([*parameter-declarations*])
        [**throws** *exception-type* [, *exception-type*…]] { … }

Description
The **throws** reserved word is used to modify a method or constructor to indicate that the code it contains may throw an instance of the specified exception (exception type).

Example

```
import java.io.*;
import java.util.*;

public class ThrowingTester {
    // The main method throws a FileNotFoundException (a checked exception)
    // if the input file used in creating the Scanner object is not present. In
    // attempting to read the first string from the input file, a
    // NoSuchElementException may be thrown if the input file is present but
    // empty.  The NoSuchElementException is an unchecked exception and can
    // be thrown (by the call to the next method, but it does not need to be listed
    // in the throws clause.
    public static void main (String[ ] args) throws FileNotFoundException {
        Scanner scan = new Scanner (new File ("input.txt"));
        System.out.println ("Hello, " + scan.next ( ));
    }
}
```

Tips
- There are two types of exceptions in Java, checked and unchecked. Checked exceptions must either be caught (using try/catch blocks) or listed in the **throws** clause in the method's definition (thereby indicating that the exception will be propagated). Unchecked exceptions are obects of the RuntimeException type (or one of its subclasses) and require no **throws** clause.
- When overriding or implementing an abstract method, you cannot add exception objects to the original method's **throws** clause.
- A method or constructor can support the throwing of multiple exceptions. To do so, add the exception types to the **throws** clause and follow each one with a comma.
- A compiler error will result if the exception type is not from the class java.lang.Throwable or a subclass of java.lang.Throwable.

See also
- catch (p. 24)
- throw (p. 60)
- try (p. 63)

transient (modifier)

Syntax

[*modifier*] **transient** *data-type variable-name*;

Description

The **transient** reserved word can be used to indicate that the instance field modified by the reserved word is not persistent when serializing the object that contains it. That is, the **transient** reserved word prevents specified instance data from being serialized.

Example

```
import java.io.Serializable;

// The SerializedStudent class contains basic information about each student.
// However, only the name and address are serialized if a SerializedStudent object
// is serialized.
public class SerializedStudent implements Serializable {
    String name;
    String address;
    transient double gpa;

    // Class and instance methods would appear here.
}
```

Tips

- Consider when to use the **transient** reserved word. Its use can decrease the amount of data serialized.

- Programmers may use the **transient** reserved word as a security measure to prevent sensitive data from being released.

See also
- java.io.Serializable (p. 85)

try (control)

Syntax

```
try {
    statement(s);
}
[ catch ( exception-type exception-identifier-name ) {
    statement(s);
} ]
[ finally {
    statement(s);
} ]
```

Description

The **try** reserved word is part of the larger **try**/catch/finally statement. Each of these reserved words encloses a block of one or more statements that are executed under certain circumstances. The **try** block is executed first, until it completes execution of its statements or an exception is thrown.

If an exception arises, each catch clause is examined one at a time, in linear order, to determine whether the thrown exception matches a particular exception type. A match is made if the type of the exception thrown can be assigned to the type being caught. If a match does occur, the statement(s) in the matching catch clause are executed.

If an exception does not arise while executing the **try** block, processing continues following the last catch block. If a finally clause is present, it is executed; otherwise, the next statement following the last catch clause is executed.

Example

```java
// This method attempts to create a new File object from the specified filename.
// The object's creation and canWrite method may result in exceptions being
// thrown for several reasons.  Thus, two catch statements are required for this
// code to be compiled.
public void checkFile (String filename) {
    try {
        File inputFile = new File (filename);
        if (inputFile.canWrite ( ))
            System.out.println ("The file: " + filename +" can be written to.");
    }
    catch (NullPointerException nullPtr) {
        System.err.println (nullPtr);
    }
    catch (SecurityException securityExpt) {
```

```
        System.err.println (securityExpt);
    }
}
```

Tips

- The finally clause is optional in the **try**/catch statement.
- A **try** block can have zero or more catch clauses associated with it as long as a different type of exception is being caught by each clause. Keep in mind that different catch clauses can have exception types that are subclasses of each other.

See also

- catch (p. 24)
- finally (p. 35)

void (data type)

Syntax

[*modifier*] **void** *method-name* ([*parameter-declarations*])
    [throws *exception-type* [, *exception-type*…]] { … }

Description

The **void** reserved word is used to denote the absence of a data value to be returned at the conclusion of a method's execution.

Example

```
// The setName method sets the character's name to the value of the cName
// parameter, but returns nothing to the calling method.
public void setName (String cName) {
    characterName = cName;
}
```

Tips

- If you use the **void** reserved word in the declaration of a method, be sure that the method lacks a return statement or the return statement (if used) lacks a value to return. The **void** reserved word prevents returning a value to the calling method.
- If you wish to return a value at the conclusion of a method's execution, use the return reserved word (see page 51).

See also

- return (p. 51)

volatile (modifier)

Syntax
[*modifier*] **volatile** *data-type variable-name* [= *initial-value-expression*];

Description
The **volatile** reserved word is used to modify an instance variable's declaration to indicate that its contents are highly subject to change by other threads. When designated as **volatile**, any attempt to read the local value of this variable (stored in the thread) causes the reading thread to ensure the correctness of the value by referring to the master copy of the variable.

Example

```
// The WorkshopSection class contains enrollment and naming information about
// each workshop offered.  Note that the currentEnrollment instance field is
// highly subject to change via threads handling workshop enrollment processing.
// Thus it is a volatile instance field.
public class WorkshopSection {
    private volatile int currentEnrollment;
    private String courseName;
    private final int maxSize = 24;
}
```

Tip
• A final variable may not also be declared **volatile**.

See also
• final (p. 34)

while (control)

Syntax
while (*boolean-expression*)
    statement;

Description
The **while** loop repeats the statement (or statements, if enclosed in braces) until the boolean expression evaluates to a "false" result. Because of its structure, the statement is not guaranteed to be executed at all. If the expression is "false" the first time it is

analyzed, the statement will never be executed. The boolean expression that controls the loop is evaluated before executing the statement portion (body) of the loop.

Examples

```
// Loop until alpha is no longer less than the target; increase alpha by two
// each time through the loop.
while (alpha < target)
    alpha = alpha + 2;
```

```
// Loop while alpha is less than the target and beta is greater than five.
// The body of the loop modifies the values of the alpha and beta variables.
while (alpha < target && beta > 5) {
    alpha++;
    beta = beta - 1;
}
```

Tips

- The statement portion of the **while** loop is not guaranteed to execute at all. Execution depends on the result of the boolean expression.

- If the boolean expression does not resolve to a boolean result ("true" or "false"), a compile-time error is generated.

- To execute multiple statements as the body of the **while** loop, enclose the statements to execute in braces, creating a statement block (see the second example).

- Be sure that the boolean expression changes as part of the body of the loop. If the value of the expression does not change, the loop will be performed endlessly. This situation is known as an *endless loop*.

- Keep in mind that the boolean expression can comprise multiple boolean expressions joined by logical operators.

- A **while** loop may contain other loops (do, for, **while**), thereby creating *nested loops*.

- Break and continue statements can be used in **while** loops.

See also

- break (p. 20)
- continue (p. 27)
- do (p. 29)

- false (p. 7)
- for (p. 38)
- true (p. 7)

Commonly Used Java API Classes and Interfaces

Boolean (class)

Description
As the wrapper class for the primitive boolean data type (see page 19), **java.lang.Boolean** is used to perform various conversions to the boolean data type as well as to provide an object wrapper for boolean data.

Class Modifiers
> public final class Boolean
> extends Object
> implements Serializable, Comparable<Boolean>

Constructors
> Boolean (boolean)
> Boolean (String)

Public Static Fields
> Boolean FALSE
> Boolean TRUE
> Class<Boolean> TYPE

Public Static Methods
> boolean getBoolean (String)
> boolean parseBoolean (String)
> String toString (boolean)
> Boolean valueOf (boolean)
> Boolean valueOf (String)

Public Instance Methods
> boolean booleanValue ( )
> int compareTo (Boolean)
> boolean equals (Object)
> int hashCode ( )
> String toString ( )

Byte (class)

Description

As the wrapper class for the primitive byte data type (see page 21), **java.lang.Byte** is used to perform various conversions to the byte data type as well as to provide an object wrapper for byte data.

Class Modifiers

    public final class Byte
    extends Number
    implements Comparable<Byte>

Constructors

    Byte (byte)
    Byte (String)

Public Static Fields

    byte MAX_VALUE
    byte MIN_VALUE
    int SIZE
    Class<Byte> TYPE

Public Static Methods

    Byte decode (String)
    byte parseByte (String)
    byte parseByte (String, int)
    String toString (byte)
    Byte valueOf (byte)
    Byte valueOf (String)
    Byte valueOf (String, int)

Public Instance Methods

    byte byteValue ( )
    int compareTo (Byte)
    double doubleValue ( )
    boolean equals (Object)
    float floatValue ( )
    int hashCode ( )
    int intValue ( )
    long longValue ( )
    short shortValue ( )
    String toString ( )

Character (class)

Description

As the wrapper class for the primitive char data type (see page 25), **java.lang.Character** is used to perform various conversions to the char data type as well as to provide an object wrapper for character data.

Class Modifiers

    public final class Character
    extends Object
    implements Serializable, Comparable<Character>

Constructor

    Character (char)

Public Static Fields

    byte COMBINING_SPACING_MARK
    byte CONNECTOR_PUNCTUATION
    byte CONTROL
    byte CURRENCY_SYMBOL
    byte DASH_PUNCTUATION
    byte DECIMAL_DIGIT_NUMBER
    byte DIRECTIONALITY_ARABIC_NUMBER
    byte DIRECTIONALITY_BOUNDARY_NEUTRAL
    byte DIRECTIONALITY_COMMON_NUMBER_SEPARATOR
    byte DIRECTIONALITY_EUROPEAN_NUMBER
    byte DIRECTIONALITY_EUROPEAN_NUMBER_SEPARATOR
    byte DIRECTIONALITY_EUROPEAN_NUMBER_TERMINATOR
    byte DIRECTIONALITY_LEFT_TO_RIGHT
    byte DIRECTIONALITY_LEFT_TO_RIGHT_EMBEDDING
    byte DIRECTIONALITY_LEFT_TO_RIGHT_OVERRIDE
    byte DIRECTIONALITY_NONSPACING_MARK
    byte DIRECTIONALITY_OTHER_NEUTRALS
    byte DIRECTIONALITY_PARAGRAPH_SEPARATOR
    byte DIRECTIONALITY_POP_DIRECTIONAL_FORMAT
    byte DIRECTIONALITY_RIGHT_TO_LEFT
    byte DIRECTIONALITY_RIGHT_TO_LEFT_ARABIC
    byte DIRECTIONALITY_RIGHT_TO_LEFT_EMBEDDING
    byte DIRECTIONALITY_RIGHT_TO_LEFT_OVERRIDE
    byte DIRECTIONALITY_SEGMENT_SEPARATOR
    byte DIRECTIONALITY_UNDEFINED
    byte DIRECTIONALITY_WHITESPACE
    byte ENCLOSING_MARK
    byte END_PUNCTUATION
    byte FINAL_QUOTE_PUNCTUATION

byte FORMAT
byte INITIAL_QUOTE_PUNCTUATION
byte LETTER_NUMBER
byte LINE_SEPARATOR
byte LOWERCASE_LETTER
byte MATH_SYMBOL
int MAX_CODE_POINT
char MAX_HIGH_SURROGATE
char MAX_LOW_SURROGATE
int MAX_RADIX
char MAX_SURROGATE
char MAX_VALUE
int MIN_CODE_POINT
char MIN_HIGH_SURROGATE
char MIN_LOW_SURROGATE
int MIN_RADIX
int MIN_SUPPLEMENTARY_CODE_POINT
char MIN_SURROGATE
char MIN_VALUE
byte MODIFIER_LETTER
byte MODIFIER_SYMBOL
byte NON_SPACING_MARK
byte OTHER_LETTER
byte OTHER_NUMBER
byte OTHER_PUNCTUATION
byte OTHER_SYMBOL
byte PARAGRAPH_SEPARATOR
byte PRIVATE_USE
int SIZE
byte SPACE_SEPARATOR
byte START_PUNCTUATION
byte SURROGATE
byte TITLECASE_LETTER
Class<Character> TYPE
byte UNASSIGNED
byte UPPERCASE_LETTER

Public Static Methods

int charCount (in)
int codePointAt (char[ ], int)
int codePointAt (char[ ], int, int)
int codePointAt (CharSequence, int)
int codePointBefore (char[ ], int)
int codePointBefore (char[ ], int, int)
int codePointBefore (CharSequence, int)
int codePointCount (char[ ], int, int)
int codePointCount (CharSequence, int, int)

int digit (char, int)
int digit (int, int)
char forDigit (int, int)
byte getDirectionality (char)
byte getDirectionality (int)
int getNumericValue (char)
int getNumericValue (int)
int getType (char)
int getType (int)
boolean isDefined (char)
boolean isDefined (int)
boolean isDigit (char)
boolean isDigit (int)
boolean isHighSurrogate (char)
boolean isIdentifierIgnorable (char)
boolean isIdentifierIgnorable (int)
boolean isISOControl (char)
boolean isISOControl (int)
boolean isJavaIdentifierPart (char)
boolean isJavaIdentifierPart (int)
boolean isJavaIdentifierStart (char)
boolean isJavaIdentifierStart (int)
boolean isJavaLetter (char)
boolean isJavaLetterOrDigit (char)
boolean isLetter (char)
boolean isLetter (int)
boolean isLetterOrDigit (char)
boolean isLetterOrDigit (int)
boolean isLowerCase (char)
boolean isLowerCase (int)
boolean isLowSurrogate (char)
boolean isMirrored (char)
boolean isMirrored (int)
boolean isSpace (char)
boolean isSpaceChar (char)
boolean isSpaceChar (int)
boolean isSupplementaryCodePoint (int)
boolean isSurrogatePair (char, char)
boolean isTitleCase (char)
boolean isTitleCase (int)
boolean isUnicodeIdentifierPart (char)
boolean isUnicodeIdentifierPart (int)
boolean isUnicodeIdentifierStart (char)
boolean isUnicodeIdentifierStart (int)
boolean isUpperCase (char)
boolean isUpperCase (int)

        boolean isValidCodePoint (int)
        boolean isWhitespace (char)
        boolean isWhitespace (int)
        int offsetByCodePoints (char[ ], int, int, int, int)
        int offsetByCodePoints (CharSequence, int, int)
        char reverseBytes (char)
        char[ ] toChars (int)
        int toChars (int, char[ ], int)
        int toCodePoint (char, char)
        char toLowerCase (char)
        int toLowerCase (int)
        String toString (char)
        char toTitleCase (char)
        int toTitleCase (int)
        char toUpperCase (char)
        int toUpperCase (int)
        Character valueOf (char)

Public Instance Methods
        char charValue ( )
        int compareTo (Character)
        boolean equals (Object)
        int hashCode ( )
        String toString ( )

Cloneable (interface)

Description
A class implements the **java.lang.Cloneable** interface to indicate that use of the clone method is permitted by an object instantiated from the implementing class. That is, the underlying class that implements the **Cloneable** interface is allowed to be cloned via the Object.clone method. The implementing class can also choose to override (or not) the clone method, providing specific functionality.

Class Modifier
        public interface Cloneable

Methods
None.

Comparable (interface)

Description
When applied to the definition of a class, the **java.lang.Comparable** interface indicates that there exists a natural ordering of instances of the class. In doing so, the programmer

implements the compareTo method, which provides a method of comparing two objects (instances of the defined class). The compareTo method always returns a negative integer, zero, or a positivie integer if this object is less than, equal to, or greater than the parameter object (T). This ability to compare two objects (and thus create an ordering) underlies the ability to sort objects.

Class Modifier
    public interface Comparable<T>

Public Static Fields
None.

Public Static Methods
None.

Public Instance Method
    int compareTo (T)

DecimalFormat (class)

Description
The **java.text.DecmialFormat** class is a subclass of java.text.NumberFormat (see page 81) that can be used to parse and format demical numbers in a variety of formats for a variety of locales. The class is generally used to format floating point numbers, integers, scientific notation values, currency, and percentages.

Class Modifiers
    public class DecimalFormat
    extends NumberFormat

Constructors
    DecimalFormat ( )
    DecimalFormat (String)
    DecimalFormat (String, DecimalFormatSymbols)

Public Static Fields
None.

Public Static Methods
None.

Public Instance Methods
    void applyLocalizedPattern (String)
    void applyPattern (String)
    Object clone ( )
    boolean equals (Object)
    StringBuffer format (double, StringBuffer, FieldPosition)
    StringBuffer format (long, StringBuffer, FieldPosition)
    StringBuffer format (Object, StringBuffer, FieldPosition)
    AttributedCharacterIterator formatToCharacterIterator (Object)

Currency getCurrency ( )
DecimalFormatSymbols getDecimalFormatSymbols ( )
int getGroupingSize ( )
int getMaximumFractionDigits ( )
int getMaximumIntegerDigits ( )
int getMinimumFractionDigits ( )
int getMinimumIntegerDigits ( )
int getMultiplier ( )
String getNegativePrefix ( )
String getNegativeSuffix ( )
String getPositivePrefix ( )
String getPositiveSuffix ( )
int hashCode ( )
boolean isDecimalSeparatorAlwaysShown ( )
boolean isParseBigDecimal ( )
Number parse (String, ParsePosition)
void setCurrency (Currency)
void setDecimalFormatSymbols (DecimalFormatSymbols)
void setDecimalSeparatorAlwaysShown (boolean)
void setGroupingSize (int)
void setMaximumFractionDigits (int)
void setMaximumIntegerDigits (int)
void setMinimumFractionDigits (int)
void setMinimumIntegerDigits (int)
void setMultiplier (int)
void setNegativePrefix (String)
void setNegativeSuffix (String)
void setParseBigDecimal (boolean)
void setPositivePrefix (String)
void setPositiveSuffix (String)
String toLocalizedPattern ( )
String toPattern ( )

Double (class)

Description

As the wrapper class for the primitive double data type (see page 30), **java.lang.Double** is used to perform various conversions to the double data type as well as to provide an object wrapper for double data.

Class Modifiers

public final class Double
extends Number
implements Comparable<Double>

Constructors

        Double (double)
        Double (String)

<u>Public Static Fields</u>
        double MAX_VALUE
        double MIN_VALUE
        double NaN
        double NEGATIVE_INFINITY
        double POSITIVE_INFINITY
        int SIZE
        Class<Double> TYPE

<u>Public Static Methods</u>
        int compare (double, double)
        long doubleToLongBits (double)
        long doubleToRawLongBits (double)
        boolean isInfinite (double)
        boolean isNaN (double)
        double longBitsToDouble (long)
        double parseDouble (String)
        String toHexString (double)
        String toString (double)
        Double valueOf (double)
        Double valueOf (String)

<u>Public Instance Methods</u>
        byte byteValue ( )
        int compareTo (Double)
        double doubleValue ( )
        boolean equals (Object)
        float floatValue ( )
        int hashCode ( )
        int intValue ( )
        boolean isInfinite ( )
        boolean isNaN ( )
        long longValue ( )
        short shortValue ( )
        String toString ( )

Float (class)

Description
As the wrapper class for the primitive float data type (see page 36), **java.lang.Float** is used to perform various conversions to the float data type as well as to provide an object wrapper for float data.

Class Modifiers

```
public final class Float
extends Number
implements Comparable<Float>
```

Constructors

```
Float (double)
Float (float)
Float (String)
```

Public Static Fields

```
float MAX_VALUE
float MIN_VALUE
float NaN
float NEGATIVE_INFINITY
float POSITIVE_INFINITY
int SIZE
Class<Float> TYPE
```

Public Static Methods

```
int compare (float, float)
int floatToIntBits (float)
int floatToRawIntBits (float)
float intBitsToFloat (int)
boolean isInfinite (float)
boolean isNaN (float)
float parseFloat (String)
String toHexString (float)
String toString (float)
Float valueOf (float)
Float valueOf (String)
```

Public Instance Methods

```
byte byteValue ( )
int compareTo (Float)
double doubleValue ( )
boolean equals (Object)
float floatValue ( )
int hashCode ( )
int intValue ( )
boolean isInfinite ( )
boolean isNaN ( )
long longValue ( )
short shortValue ( )
String toString ( )
```

Integer (class)

Description

As the wrapper class for the primitive int data type (see page 43), **java.lang.Integer** is used to perform various conversions to the int data type as well as to provide an object wrapper for int data.

Class Modifiers

    public final class Integer
    extends Number
    implements Comparable<Integer>

Constructors

    Integer (int)
    Integer (String)

Public Static Fields

    int MAX_VALUE
    int MIN_VALUE
    int SIZE
    Class<Integer> TYPE

Public Static Methods

    int bitCount (int)
    Integer decode (String)
    Integer getInteger (String)
    Integer getInteger (String, int)
    Integer getInteger (String, Integer)
    int highestOneBit (int)
    int lowestOneBit (int)
    int numberOfLeadingZeros (int)
    int numberOfTrailingZeros (int)
    int parseInt (String)
    int parseInt (String, int)
    int reverse (int)
    int reverseBytes (int)
    int rotateLeft (int, int)
    int rotateRight (int, int)
    int signum (int)
    String toBinaryString (int)
    String toHexString (int)
    String toOctalString (int)
    String toString (int)
    String toString (int, int)
    Integer valueOf (int)
    Integer valueOf (String)

Integer valueOf (String, int)

Public Instance Methods
byte byteValue ( )
int compareTo (Integer)
double doubleValue ( )
boolean equals (Object)
float floatValue ( )
int hashCode ( )
int intValue ( )
long longValue ( )
short shortValue ( )
String toString ( )

Iterator (interface)

Description
The **java.util.Iterator** class is an interface that is implemented by an underlying class that defines a collection of objects. The **Iterator** provides a mechanism to move the collection over one item at a time. Iterators do not remove the objects from the underlying collection.

Class Modifier
public interface Iterator<E>

Public Static Fields
None.

Public Static Methods
None.

Public Instance Methods
boolean hasNext ( )
E next ( )
void remove ( )

Long (class)

Description
As the wrapper class for the primitive long data type (see page 45), **java.lang.Long** is used to perform various conversions to the long data type as well as to provide an object wrapper for long data.

Class Modifiers
public final class Long
extends Number
implements Comparable<Long>

Constructors

    Long (long)
    Long (String)

Public Static Fields

    long MAX_VALUE
    long MIN_VALUE
    int SIZE
    Class<Long> TYPE

Public Static Methods

    int bitCount (long)
    Long decode (String)
    Long getLong (String)
    Long getLong (String, long)
    Long getLong (String, Long)
    long highestOneBit (long)
    long lowestOneBit (long)
    int numberOfLeadingZeros (long)
    int numberOfTrailingZeros (long)
    long parseLong (String)
    long parseLong (String, int)
    long reverse (long)
    long reverseBytes (long)
    long rotateLeft (long, int)
    long rotateRight (long, int)
    int signum (long)
    String toBinaryString (long)
    String toHexString (long)
    String toOctalString (long)
    String toString (long)
    String toString (long, int)
    Long valueOf (long)
    Long valueOf (String)
    Long valueOf (String, int)

Public Instance Methods

    byte byteValue ( )
    int compareTo (Long)
    double doubleValue ( )
    boolean equals (Object)
    float floatValue ( )
    int hashCode ( )
    int intValue ( )
    long longValue ( )
    short shortValue ( )
    String toString ( )

Math (class)

Description
The **java.lang.Math** contains a large number of mathematical operations and functions. The **Math** class exists solely to provide static fields and methods for general-purpose use to other classes (both API and user-defined).

Class Modifiers
```
public final class Math
extends Object
```

Constructors
None.

Public Static Fields
```
double E
double PI
```

Public Static Methods
```
double abs (double)
float abs (float)
int abs (int)
long abs (long)
double acos (double)
double asin (double)
double atan (double)
double atan2 (double, double)
double cbrt (double)
double ceil (double)
double cos (double)
double cosh (double)
double exp (double)
double expm1 (double)
double floor (double)
double hypot (double, double)
double IEEEremainder (double, double)
double log (double)
double log10 (double)
double log1p (double)
double max (double, double)
float max (float, float)
int max (int, int)
long max (long, long)
double min (double, double)
float min (float, float)
int min (int, int)
```

```
long min (long, long)
double pow (double, double)
double random ( )
double rint (double)
long round (double)
int round (float)
double signum (double)
float signum (float)
double sin (double)
double sinh (double)
double sqrt (double)
double tan (double)
double tanh (double)
double toDegrees (double)
double toRadians (double)
double ulp (double)
float ulp (float)
```

Public Instance Method
None.

NumberFormat (class)

Description
The **java.text.NumberFormat** class is used to parse and format a variety of numbers, given a system's locale.

Class Modifiers
```
public abstract class NumberFormat
extends Format
```

Constructor
```
NumberFormat ( )
```

Public Static Fields
```
int FRACTION_FIELD
int INTEGER_FIELD
```

Public Static Methods
```
Locale[ ] getAvailableLocales ( )
NumberFormat getCurrencyInstance ( )
NumberFormat getCurrencyInstance (Locale)
NumberFormat getInstance ( )
NumberFormat getInstance (Locale)
NumberFormat getIntegerInstance ( )
NumberFormat getIntegerInstance (Locale)
NumberFormat getNumberInstance ( )
NumberFormat getNumberInstance (Locale)
```

NumberFormat getPercentInstance ( )
NumberFormat getPercentInstance (Locale)

Public Instance Methods

Object clone ( )
boolean equals (Object)
String format (double)
String format (long)
StringBuffer format (Object, StringBuffer, FieldPosition)
Currency getCurrency ( )
int getMaximumFractionDigits ( )
int getMaximumIntegerDigits ( )
int getMinimumFractionDigits ( )
int getMinimumIntegerDigits ( )
int hashCode ( )
boolean isGroupingUsed ( )
boolean isParseIntegerOnly ( )
Number parse (String)
Object parseObject (String, ParsePosition)
void setCurrency (Currency)
void setGroupingUsed (boolean)
void setMaximumFractionDigits (int)
void setMaximumIntegerDigits (int)
void setMinimumFractionDigits (int)
void setMinimumIntegerDigits (int)
void setParseIntegerOnly (boolean)

Abstract Methods

StringBuffer format (double, StringBuffer, FieldPosition)
StringBuffer format (long, StringBuffer, FieldPosition)
Number parse (String, ParsePosition)

Object (class)

Description

The **java.lang.Object** is the root superclass for all classes in the Java language. It contains methods applicable to every object in the Java language.

Class Modifier

public class Object

Constructor

Object ( )

Public Static Fields
None.

Public Static Methods

None.

Public Instance Methods
    boolean equals (Object)
    Class<? extends Object> getClass ( )
    int hashCode ( )
    void notify ( )
    void notifyAll ( )
    String toString ( )
    void wait ( )
    void wait (long)
    void wait (long, int)

Protected Instance Methods
    Object clone ( )
    void finalize ( )

Random (class)

Description

The **java.util.Random** class is used to create pseudo-random numbers in a variety of formats. The sequence of values generated is determined by the seed value set by the constructor (or the setSeed method). **Random** objects that are based on the same seed value produce identical sequences of values (hence the pseudo-random nature).

Class Modifiers
    public class Random
    extends Object
    implements Serializable

Constructors
    Random ( )
    Random (long)

Public Static Fields
None.

Public Static Methods
None.

Public Instance Methods
    boolean nextBoolean ( )
    void nextBytes (byte[ ])
    double nextDouble ( )
    float nextFloat ( )
    double nextGaussian ( )
    int nextInt ( )
    int nextInt (int)
    long nextLong ( )

void setSeed (long)

Protected Instance Method
    int next (int)

Scanner (class)

Description
The **java.util.Scanner** class provides string tokenization to a variety of input streams (files, System.in, and so on).

Class Modifiers
    public final class Scanner
    extends Object
    implements Iterator<String>

Constructors
    Scanner (File)
    Scanner (File, String)
    Scanner (InputStream)
    Scanner (InputStream, String)
    Scanner (Readable)
    Scanner (ReadableByteChannel)
    Scanner (ReadableByteChannel, String)
    Scanner (String)

Public Static Fields
None.

Public Static Methods:
None.

Public Instance Methods
    void close ( )
    Pattern delimiter ( )
    String findInLine (Pattern)
    String findInLine (String)
    String findWithinHorizon (Pattern, int)
    String findWithinHorizon (String, int)
    boolean hasNext ( )
    boolean hasNext (Pattern)
    boolean hasNext (String)
    boolean hasNextBigDecimal ( )
    boolean hasNextBigInteger ( )
    boolean hasNextBigInteger (int)
    boolean hasNextBoolean ( )
    boolean hasNextByte ( )
    boolean hasNextByte (int)

boolean hasNextDouble ( )
boolean hasNextFloat ( )
boolean hasNextInt ( )
boolean hasNextInt (int)
boolean hasNextLine ( )
boolean hasNextLong ( )
boolean hasNextLong (int)
boolean hasNextShort ( )
boolean hasNextShort (int)
IOException ioException ( )
Locale locale ( )
MatchResult match ( )
String next ( )
String next (Pattern)
String next (String)
BigDecimal nextBigDecimal ( )
BigInteger nextBigInteger ( )
BigInteger nextBigInteger (int)
boolean nextBoolean ( )
byte nextByte ( )
byte nextByte (int)
double nextDouble ( )
float nextFloat ( )
int nextInt ( )
int nextInt (int)
String nextLine ( )
long nextLong ( )
long nextLong (int)
short nextShort ( )
short nextShort (int)
int radix ( )
void remove ( )
Scanner skip (Pattern)
Scanner skip (String)
String toString ( )
Scanner useDelimiter (Pattern)
Scanner useDelimiter (String)
Scanner useLocale (Locale)
Scanner useRadix (int)

Serializable (interface)

Description

A class can implement the **java.io.Serializable** interface to show that the class has been designed to have its contents made persistent by using Java Serialization. By marking a class as having implemented the Serializable interface, an instance of the class may be written as a sequence of bytes to an output stream (and read back in again, recreating the original object(s)).

Class Modifier
    public interface Serializable

Methods
None.

Short (class)

Description

As the wrapper class for the primitive short data type (see page 52), **java.lang.Short** is used to perform various conversions to the short data type as well as to provide an Object wrapper for short data.

Class Modifiers
    public final class Short
    extends Number
    implements Comparable<Short>

Constructors
    Short (short)
    Short (String)

Public Static Fields
    long MAX_VALUE
    long MIN_VALUE
    int SIZE
    Class<Short> TYPE

Public Static Methods
    Short decode (String)
    short parseShort (String)
    short parseShort (String, int)
    short reverseBytes (short)
    String toString (short)
    Short valueOf (short)
    Short valueOf (String)
    Short valueOf (String, int)

Public Instance Methods
    byte byteValue ( )
    int compareTo (Short)
    double doubleValue ( )
    boolean equals (Object)
    float floatValue ( )

```
int hashCode ( )
int intValue ( )
long longValue ( )
short shortValue ( )
String toString ( )
```

String (class)

Description
The **java.lang.String** class is used to represent and modify character strings (sequences of multiple characters).

Class Modifiers
```
public final class String
extends Object
implements Serializable, Comparable<String>, CharSequence
```

Constructors
```
String ( )
String (byte[ ])
String (byte[ ], int)
String (byte[ ], int, int)
String (byte[ ], int, int, int)
String (byte[ ], int, int, String)
String (byte[ ], String)
String (char[ ])
String (char[ ], int, int)
String (int[ ], int, int)
String (String)
String (StringBuffer)
String (StringBuilder)
```

Public Static Field
```
Comparator<String> CASE_INSENSITIVE_ORDER
```

Public Static Methods
```
String copyValueOf (char[ ])
String copyValueOf (char[ ], int, int)
String format (Locale, String, Object...)
String format (String, Object...)
String valueOf (boolean)
String valueOf (char)
String valueOf (char[ ])
String valueOf (char[ ], int, int)
String valueOf (double)
String valueOf (float)
String valueOf (int)
```

        String valueOf (long)
        String valueOf (Object)

Public Instance Methods

        char charAt (int)
        int codePointAt (int)
        int codePointBefore (int)
        int codePointCount (int, int)
        int compareTo (String)
        int compareToIgnoreCase (String)
        String concat (String)
        boolean contains (CharSequence)
        boolean contentEquals (StringBuffer)
        boolean contentEquals (StringBuffer)
        boolean endsWith (String)
        boolean equals (Object)
        boolean equalsIgnoreCase (String)
        byte[ ] getBytes ( )
        void getBytes (int, int, byte[ ], int)
        byte[ ] getBytes (String)
        void getChars (int, int, char[ ], int)
        int hashCode ( )
        int indexOf (int)
        int indexOf (int, int)
        int indexOf (String)
        int indexOf (String, int)
        String intern ( )
        int lastIndexOf (int)
        int lastIndexOf (int, int)
        int lastIndexOf (String)
        int lastIndexOf (String, int)
        int length ( )
        boolean matches (String)
        boolean regionMatches (boolean, int, String, int, int)
        boolean regionMatches (int, String, int, int)
        String replace (char, char)
        String replace (String, String)
        String replace(CharSequence, CharSequence)
        String replaceAll (String, String)
        String replaceFirst (String, String)
        String[ ] split (String)
        String[ ] split (String, int)
        boolean startsWith (String)
        boolean startsWith (String, int)
        CharSequence subSequence (int, int)
        String substring (int)
        String substring (int, int)

char[ ] toCharArray ( )
String toLowerCase ( )
String toLowerCase (Locale)
String toString ( )
String toUpperCase ( )
String toUpperCase (Locale)
String trim ( )

System (class)

Description

The **java.lang.System** class provides a variety of useful methods for obtaining information about your system. This class cannot be instantiated.

Class Modifiers

public final class System
extends Object

Constructors
None.

Public Static Fields

PrintStream err
InputStream in
PrintStream out

Public Static Methods

void arraycopy (Object, int, Object, int, int)
String clearProperty (String)
long currentTimeMillis ( )
void exit (int)
void gc ( )
Map<String, String> getenv ( )
String getenv (String)
Properties getProperties ( )
String getProperty (String)
String getProperty (String, String)
SecurityManager getSecurityManager ( )
int identityHashCode (Object)
Channel inheritedChannel ( )
void load (String)
void loadLibrary (String)
String mapLibraryName (String)
long nanoTime ( )
void runFinalization ( )
void runFinalizersOnExit (boolean)
void setErr (PrintStream)

void setIn (InputStream)
void setOut (PrintStream)
void setProperties (Properties)
String setProperty (String, String)
void setSecurityManager (SecurityManager)

Public Instance Methods
None.

INDEX